PENGUIN BOOKS

REDISCOVERING DHARAVI: STORIES FROM ASIA'S LARGEST SLUM

Kalpana Sharma has been a journalist since 1972 and has worked with *Himmat*, *The Indian Express*, *The Times of India* and *The Hindu*. She has specialized in writing on environmental and developmental issues, with a special focus on the concerns of women. With Ammu Joseph, she has written and edited *Whose News? The Media and Women's Issues*. For her column, 'The Other Half', which first appeared in *The Indian Express* (and appears currently in *The Hindu*, where she is a Deputy Editor), Kalpana Sharma was awarded the Chameli Devi Jain Award for an Outstanding Woman Journalist in 1987. She lives in Mumbai.

REDISCOVERING DHARAVI

Stories From Asia's Largest Slum

Kalpana Sharma

PENGUIN BOOKS

Penguin Books India (P) Ltd., 11 Community Centre, Panchsheel Park, New Delhi 110 017, India
Penguin Books Ltd., 27 Wrights Lane, London W8 5TZ, UK
Penguin Putnam Inc., 375 Hudson Street, New York, NY 10014, USA
Penguin Books Australia Ltd., Ringwood, Victoria, Australia
Penguin Books Canada Ltd., 10 Alcorn Avenue, Suite 300, Toronto, Ontario, M4V 3B2, Canada
Penguin Books (NZ) Ltd., Cnr Rosedale and Airborne Roads, Albany, Auckland, New Zealand

First published by Penguin Books India 2000

Copyright © Kalpana Sharma 2000

10 9 8 7 6 5 4 3 2

Typeset in *Sabon Roman* by SÜRYA, New Delhi
Printed at Chaman Offset Printers, New Delhi

To

my father
and
the people of Dharavi

Contents

List of photographs in chapter openings

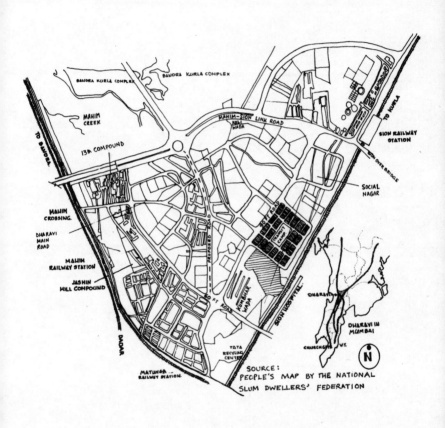

SOURCE:
PEOPLE'S MAP BY THE NATIONAL
SLUM DWELLERS' FEDERATION

Preface

This book would not have been written if the people of Dharavi had not welcomed me into their homes, extended their hospitality, and shared their stories and their dreams with me. Many of them are featured in this book, many more are not. But to each one of them I owe a debt of gratitude for what they taught me about their attitude to life.

For instance, when I asked young Selvy from Kamaraj Nagar, who is studying to be a chartered accountant, whether they have a water problem, she cheerfully replied, 'Not at all. See those drums? We have plenty of water!' This is the attitude that makes Dharavi what it is, an approach to life that refuses to accept defeat.

Of all the people I spoke to in Dharavi, a special word of thanks to Amina and Mariam, who were always available to me whenever I went to Dharavi to double-check a fact, or to follow up on information I had earlier gathered.

I would never have met Amina, or Haji Shamsuddin, or Eklakh if Sushobha Barve, who has worked indefatigably for communal peace, had not introduced me to them. It is because of the confidence all these people had in 'Barve-bai' that I was given entry into their homes and their confidences. Sushobha has worked in Dharavi through the 1992-93 riots, often spending nights there, and since then to nurture the Mohalla Committee movement there and elsewhere in Mumbai. As a result, everywhere we went, doors opened, people were more than willing to talk. I am deeply conscious of the fact that I could not have expected this had I gone on my own. Sushobha spent many hours with me, finding people, setting up appointments, helping me understand the complicated relationships between people, between groups. This book is as much her work as it is mine.

The president of the National Slum Dwellers' Federation, A. Jockin, who was awarded the Ramon Magsaysay Award for International Understanding for the year 2000, has always helped me to find a perspective on issues relating to the urban poor. His simple, uncomplicated yet wise approach to the problems that he lives with every day of his life has helped me to discard sentimental middle-class attitudes towards the urban poor and, instead, to see them as people like us who can think out and plan their own future. One of the first people with whom I discussed this book was Jockin. I thank him for the time he spent in explaining the genesis of a place like Dharavi.

A source of constant encouragement has been my father, who patiently read through all my half-baked drafts, made endless cups of tea for me, and gave me silent support as I struggled to make sense of the information I had gathered.

I also want to thank my friends Sujata Patel, Sharda Ugra and Sheela Patel, who also read through parts of the book and gave me helpful suggestions, and Arvind Krishnaswamy, who helped with the Tamil translation.

Rafeeq Ellias and Ayesha Taleyarkhan, professional photographers who also happen to be friends, were enthusiastic about shooting the photographs for this book. I am deeply indebted to them for the time they gave to the job—no easy task at the best of times but made more difficult as they had to find bright days during an exceptionally heavy monsoon season in Mumbai.

And, finally, I thank Krishan Chopra and Kalpana Joshi of Penguin India, who worked with me on editing and finalizing the manuscript, and my former colleague, David Davidar, who constantly reminded me of my promise that I would, one day, write a book that he would publish.

Mumbai, May 2000   *Kalpana Sharma*

Introduction

Through the light from a door leading to a dimly-lit narrow room, you see a white-haired man intently turning a potter's wheel, fashioning a garden pot from a lump of clay. Ramjibhai Pithabhai Patel, a sixty-five-year-old Kumbhar, lives in Dharavi, Mumbai. From early morning he is at work, pausing rarely for a break. Beyond the room, whose walls are covered with calendars and pictures of a pantheon of Hindu gods, are the kilns in which his pots will soon be placed. A pall of smoke hangs over the courtyard as a worker stamps on a mound of clay, preparing it for Ramjibhai and other potters.

'When I was growing up, this was an open space. We could see Mahim station from here. People used to be afraid to come to Dharavi. They thought of it as a jungle,' recalls Ramjibhai. He lives in Kumbharwada, a settlement where Kumbhars who fled from the drought and famine in Saurashtra, Gujarat, many decades ago live and work today.

The men and women of Ramjibhai's generation,

who remember what Dharavi was like fifty years ago, are few. Once Dharavi was a swamp, a fishing village. Today, it is a slum, or rather, a collection of slums. Once it was open marshy land with tall grass. Today, there is barely any open space in this seething, compacted spread of energy, enterprise, deprivation and desperation which epitomizes the crisis of all fast-growing Indian cities, not just Mumbai. It draws attention to the urgent need to find space and solutions for the growing numbers of the urban poor.

This heart-shaped spread of settlements, which today has the dubious reputation of being 'Asia's largest slum', is located between Mumbai's two main suburban railway lines, Western and Central Railway. These are the virtual lifelines of Mumbai, transporting thousands of people from one end of the metropolis to the other. Dharavi is literally sandwiched between the two sets of tracks. To its west are Mahim and Bandra, to its north lies the Mithi river which empties out into the Arabian Sea through the Mahim creek, and to its east and south are Sion and Matunga. Mahim, Matunga and Sion stations mark its three corners.

When people in Mumbai ask me, why a book on Dharavi, on a slum, I tell them that I am writing about their city, about Mumbai, about a reality which many would prefer to ignore. This is the reality of half of our city, of people who have been forced by chance and circumstances to live for generations in subhuman conditions. It is the story of men and women who have survived despite our indifference, despite the hostility of the State, people who are also citizens of Mumbai.

I set out to write about Dharavi from several

perspectives. First, from that of a journalist interested in people. Too often places are known as geographical dots on a map; as historical landmarks or as politically significant areas. Dharavi is all these but above all it is an extraordinary mix of the most unusual people. Their lives are the story of Dharavi; their lives are Dharavi. This is what I wanted to record.

Second, Dharavi's history and growth illustrate graphically the problems with urban planning by default. Governments first ignore the existence of slums and try and get rid of them through demolitions. When this does not succeed, and slums emerge as settled areas through the efforts of their 'illegal' occupants, they are 'recognized'. After this, selectively, some services are offered, such as water and sanitation and even 'redevelopment'. But slum-dwellers are never allowed to forget that they have no legal status. Thus, when the land on which slums are located becomes valuable property, people are pushed out yet again, to another uninhabitable piece of land, to another slum.

The consequence of such an ad hoc and short-sighted approach towards the housing needs of the urban poor is evident in every Indian city where, roughly, between half and three quarters of the population lives in slums or in sub-standard houses.

Despite these policies, poor people survive. They have found ways to get water, even if water is not supplied, to build houses even when there is no security of tenure and no financial help, and to find work.

Many times they do not survive, specially when nature also turns against them. Every year, the poor in Mumbai suffer incredible hardships during the monsoons.

Their settlements—usually located in low-lying areas—
are awash in rivers of sewage and rainwater that gush
through their congested lanes. For days on end, the
muck does not clear.

The worst off are those who have perched
precariously on hillsides or along water pipes. As we
saw in the monsoon of 2000, they are the first victims
of a heavy monsoon. Their homes collapse, their children
fall into the rising water, they are cut off for days as all
the land around their settlements gets inundated.

On 12 July 2000, when Mumbai saw 251 mm of
rain in just nine hours, the city came to a standstill.
Trains stopped. Streets were submerged. And an entire
hillside in the north-eastern suburb of Ghatkopar came
tumbling down, crushing below it scores of hutments
that had perched on it for several decades. Within
minutes, the lives of over seventy men, women and
children were obliterated.

This ghastly tragedy illustrated the desperation of
poor people in the city who have nowhere to live. When
those who survived were asked why they had not
moved, despite warnings, every person said, 'Where
could we go?' Yet, the central message from the tragedy
escaped the politicians—that if the State has no policy
to house its poor, they have no option but to occupy
any vacant space that is available, no matter how
dangerous.

Despite their precarious existence, however, in many
slums enterprises and industries flourish even though
they are deemed 'illegal' because they do not conform
either to industrial location norms, or to working
conditions required of such units. The State does not
move against them—turning a blind eye to their apparent

illegality because it must know that they provide gainful employment to millions of people.

You see all this in Dharavi. No one complains about the kind of enterprises that operate there day and night because they give jobs to successive waves of rural migrants till they can move on to something else. Many begin as workers and end up 'owners' of small factories. Dharavi illustrates how the State, in fact, endorses and encourages illegality with one hand, while trying to curb it with the other.

Oddly enough, it is this deemed illegal status of informal settlements like Dharavi that makes people presume that they are breeding grounds for criminals and other 'antisocial' elements. It is also assumed that the spatial layout of such settlements, where people have no place to breathe and live literally on top of each other, exacerbates tensions—communal, class or caste.

Dharavi explodes these myths. It demonstrates that crime is the consequence of the State's policies and not inherent in the nature of people who are forced to live in slums. It also reveals that despite an explosive mix of different communities that live in impossibly crowded surroundings, there have been relatively few incidents of violence between the different groups. There are tensions but people have worked out ways of resolving them which do not involve the police or the State. Until 1992, Dharavi was one of the places in Mumbai to have witnessed hardly any communal clashes despite almost an equal number of Muslims and Hindus living in close proximity to one another. Things changed after 6 December 1992 and the demolition of the Babri Masjid.

Thus, a closer look at a place like Dharavi is

essential because it provides an insight into issues that relate generally to the place of the poor in the rapidly expanding Indian cities.

Dharavi's birth

In popular imagination, Dharavi is a dirty, pest-ridden locality without basic services where thousands of people live in subhuman conditions. It is partly this—but it is much more. For the truth of the matter is that Dharavi, a settlement with almost one million people (there is a considerable gap between 'official' and 'unofficial' population figures because of a large, unregistered, floating population), spread over 175 hectares, is a bustling collection of contiguous settlements, each with its own distinct identity. The dividing line between these settlements is sometimes a *nallah*, sometimes a small road, sometimes a wall—constructed hastily at times of conflict.

The real dividing lines are based on the history of migration patterns in the city of Mumbai, on the State's policies of dealing with the urban poor, of village industries that have translocated in an urban setting and of language, religion and region.

Dharavi was not born yesterday. It is not a 'slum' in the sense that one refers to the so-called 'illegal' or informal settlements of the urban poor found in every Indian city. It existed when Mumbai was still Bombay, when the city comprised seven islands separated by the Mahim creek from the hinterland.

In the *Gazetteer of Bombay City and Island* (1909), Dharavi is mentioned as one of the 'six great Koliwadas of Bombay', that is, of the fishing communities. The original inhabitants of Dharavi were the Kolis, the fisherfolk, who lived at the edge of the creek that came in from the Arabian Sea.

From the beginning of the eighteenth century, by accident and design, some of the swamps and the salt pan lands separating the islands that formed Bombay were reclaimed. A dam at Sion, which was adjacent to Dharavi, also hastened the process of joining separate islands into one long, tapered land mass. Thus began the transformation of the island city of Bombay. In the process, the creek dried up, Dharavi's fisherfolk were deprived of their traditional source of sustenance, and the newly emerged land from the marshes provided space for new communities to move in.

The history of Dharavi's development is also closely entwined with the migratory pattern which has marked the city of Mumbai. The migrants could be roughly divided into two broad categories. The first were people from Maharashtra, and in particular from the Konkan coast, as well as some groups from Gujarat. These communities first settled in south Bombay, on vacant plots of land. As the city grew, the authorities could not tolerate the existence of these informal settlements. Entire communities were pushed out of south Bombay to what was then the edge of the city—Dharavi. Thus, the potters from Saurashtra settled in south Bombay had to relocate twice before they were allocated land in Dharavi to establish what is till today called Kumbharwada. As a result, a part of the history of Dharavi is closely linked to the State's policy of demolitions—a policy that it continues to pursue even today, albeit in a modified form.

The other settlers were direct migrants to the city, many of them trained in a trade or a craft. Muslim tanners from Tamil Nadu migrated and set up the leather tanning industry. It was located in Dharavi because the abattoir was close by, in Bandra. Other artisans, like the embroidery workers from Uttar Pradesh, started the ready-made garments trade. From Tamil Nadu, workers joined the flourishing business of making savouries and sweets like chakli, chiki and mysore pak.

As a result, Dharavi today is an amazing mosaic of villages and townships from all over India. As the Kolis and the new migrants reclaimed and developed the land on which they lived, their kin would join them. The tanning industry grew into a thriving leather trade. Today, only a handful of the old tanneries exist but the public face of the leather trade can be seen in air-conditioned leather showrooms on the main road which display every conceivable designer label. Small-time garments manufacturers, working out of their homes with a couple of machines, expanded their units into export-oriented garment 'factories'.

As long as Dharavi was at the edge of what constituted the city of Bombay, the city authorities could ignore its existence. It was a suitable site to send communities of 'illegals' from other parts of the city as the land on which they squatted was required for other purposes. As Bombay expanded in the nineteenth century and its population grew with new industries, such as textiles, coming up in the island city, the pressure on land increased. The city began to expand into the hinterland. As a result, Dharavi became much more central; it was not at the edge of the city as in the past. Ironically, this heart-shaped settlement is now located literally in the heart of Mumbai.

This new, accidental, and more important location of Dharavi has been crucial to its recent development. Dharavi's importance was finally recognized in the mid-1980s. As a result, the government cracked down on crime and illicit liquor brewing (until then, it had turned a blind eye, allowing this illegal trade to flourish under its very nose) and, for the first time, funds were offered to make the place more liveable. On a visit to Bombay, during the Congress Party's centenary celebrations in 1985, the then Prime Minister, Rajiv Gandhi, visited Dharavi. He sanctioned a grant of Rs 100 crore to Bombay, of which a substantial amount was allocated to Dharavi. Some of this money went towards the Prime Minister's Grant Project (PMGP), which was the first attempt to redevelop parts of Dharavi.

Thus began Dharavi's transformation, albeit a superficial one. The appearance of high-rise buildings on Dharavi's periphery accelerated greatly during the latter part of the 1990s, after the Slum Redevelopment Scheme was launched by the Shiv Sena-Bharatiya Janata Party government in 1995. If the scheme had been better devised, it is possible that many more such buildings would have been constructed by the year 2000. Instead, there were more schemes on paper than on the ground. The successful schemes were those where communities were genuinely involved in the planning and implementation of the project. The paper schemes were those where builders rushed in, hoping to make huge profits, and left just as swiftly when they realized that the project was not half as lucrative. Profit was the only motive, not philanthropy.

These efforts to redevelop Dharavi—by reorganizing its informal settlements and converting them into formal housing—illustrate the complexities of slum renewal and redevelopment. 'Redeveloping' a place like Dharavi is no easy matter, as successive governments and planning authorities have discovered.

People's history

Settlements like Dharavi emerge from the life stories of the people who inhabit them. They are not the planned townships much desired as a solution to urban blight. The way they grow merges with the lives of the men and women who imbue them with a personality.

Like many others in Mumbai, I too did not know precisely what and where was this 'slum' called Dharavi. I discovered it, so to speak, during the 1992-93 communal riots that followed the demolition of the Babri Masjid in Ayodhya by Hindu fanatics who insisted it was the site of a Ram temple. As a journalist, I had to visit Dharavi frequently to report on the riots which stretched out over several weeks in December 1992 and January 1993 and which paralysed Mumbai as never before.

The Dharavi I saw then was completely different from what I came to know later. Then, the streets were deserted. For days on end, the entire area was under curfew. People were afraid to speak out. They wanted to know your credentials before they would talk to you.

One of the questions you were often asked was whether you were a Hindu or a Muslim.

The Dharavi I came to know while working on this book was a bustling, busy, chaotic settlement where nothing stood still. And no one stood still. No one asked me whether I was a Hindu or a Muslim. Almost everyone was willing to talk, and to talk at length. And most people I met had a story that could make a book on its own. I discovered then that, above all, Dharavi is the intermingling of the stories of its residents—ordinary and extraordinary—of their lives, their histories and the history of the city of Mumbai.

Take Haji Shamsuddin from Tirukoyoor in North Arcot, Tamil Nadu. Today, he lives in one of Dharavi's new high-rise buildings. But he began his life in Bombay living in one of the huts that then constituted the informal housing stock in Dharavi. He started his career as a rice smuggler (bringing in rice from the outer suburbs of present-day Mumbai to the island city), moved on to working in a printing press and, finally, began making chiki (peanut brittle) that is A-1 not just in name (that is the brand name) but also in the consistent quality which has been maintained.

Similarly, Selvaraj is from Tirunelvelli district. Like other Tamil migrants to Bombay, he came to stay, not just to visit. Many from his district worked in the tanneries. They were also involved in the illegal liquor trade in the 1960s. Today, they have branched out into other trades including finished leather goods, foodstuff like chiki and idli batter, and white-collar jobs in banks and multinational companies. If you visit his part of Dharavi, you will forget you are in Mumbai. It is a skilful re-creation of a village in Tamil Nadu. While the children look scrubbed and clean as they get ready to go to school each morning, the women wear fresh flowers in their hair. Their houses too have the same scrubbed look.

Then there is Amina, who lives in the crowded, winding lanes of Muslim Nagar, off 90 Feet Road, one of the main roads in Dharavi. Her claim to fame is the role she played in putting out potential fires during the 1992-93 communal riots in Mumbai. Amina represents a band of brave and exceptional women in Dharavi who have worked fearlessly and, at considerable personal risk, helped people during times of crisis, cutting across religion and region. This is particularly remarkable in the post-Babri Masjid period when old friendships, based on shared difficulties as a community of urban poor, were shattered by identity politics which branded people according to their religious beliefs. Women like Amina rose above all this.

A changing landscape

You can enter Dharavi through several different routes. It is conveniently located within easy reach of three stations, Matunga and Mahim on the Western Railway and Sion on the Central Railway. Thanks to the new developments, it is also linked by two link roads that connect east and west Mumbai—Sion and Mahim. Mumbai's traditional development has been along a north-south axis. The building of these link roads represented the beginning of a transition that aims to move the focus away from south Mumbai to the centre of Mumbai, closer to Dharavi.

It is this shift in focus that marked the start of the changes that Dharavi has witnessed in just over a decade. In this decade, an area that was left unsewered had sewer lines installed, at least on its periphery. Water lines were laid and roads widened. Thus, today 60 Feet Road and 90 Feet Road are the two main roads that cut across Dharavi. (They are so named because of their ostensible width.) The original Dharavi Main Road remains 'main' only in name; in fact it is little more than a dirt track.

Furthermore, the concept of 'slum redevelopment'— which meant recognizing the fact that poor people live in a particular place because it is also where they work—was attempted. Today, this is an accepted policy in dealing with the urban poor. One hopes future governments will learn from the pitfalls of past efforts. Unfortunately, institutional memory in India is practically non-existent and each new group in power attempts to reinvent the wheel.

If Dharavi is accepted as a slum, even though it comprises several settlements merging into one another, its very size is daunting. It has an enormous spread, almost that of a small township. What is even more daunting is the density of population, an estimated 18,000 persons per acre. In this densely packed area you find twenty-seven temples, eleven mosques and six churches. The oldest mosque, Badi Masjid, was built in 1887, Ganesh Mandir was constructed in 1913 and the cross in Koliwada dates back to 1850. According to local legend, the temple of Khamba Deo, whom the Hindu Kolis worship, is at least 200 years old.

At one end of Dharavi is the Rehwa Fort, popularly known as Kala Killa. You cannot see it for the houses around it. But there it stands, a stone rampart or tower. The legend on the wall reads: 'Built By Order of the Honorable Horn Esq. President and Governor of Bombay in 1737.' It is signed 'Engineer.' The settlement that has grown around the fort hardly cares about its history. At its base children play cricket, on its ramparts are piles of plastic bags, the indestructible urban scourge.

Despite some redevelopment, the overall landscape of Dharavi remains that of low-rise structures, most of them not arranged in any particular order. The huts came first, the roads, lanes, drains came afterwards. But there is an order in the apparent disorder, an order which you can only really know about if you live in one of these lanes.

Localities differ greatly, not just in terms of the communities that live there, but by the history of their development. There are, for instance, many 'settled' chawls. These are low-rise buildings which have tiled roofs and single rooms opening out on the same side. Some of these were built by the municipality, others by owners of the land. In some cases, stables were converted into chawls. Today, these chawls are surrounded by unplanned structures. It is only when you chance upon them that you realize that some of them are over eighty years old and actually have a form and a plan.

Then there is the Transit Camp. As the name suggests, these were temporary structures built by the government to relocate people who came in the way of expanding one of Dharavi's main roads, or for laying the sewer and water pipes. Today, this has become another settlement. The temporary structures have been strengthened. People have built on them. You see houses which are two storeys high going up to 24 feet while government regulation allows only 14 feet, a 9-foot-high room with a 5-foot-high loft.

On private lands, particularly those vacated by the tanneries that moved out when the government ordered them to do so, high-rise buildings have been constructed that sit oddly in the middle of the generally slum-like surroundings. Vaibhav, built by the Rahejas on land vacated by the Western India Tanneries, the oldest tannery in Dharavi, has an odd mixture of residents, all of whom have once lived in some other part of Dharavi. Today, they are rich enough to afford a flat in this building.

The oldest of the high-rises is Diamond Apartments. It overlooks Mahim station on one side, and on the other, all of Dharavi and beyond. From the eleventh-floor apartment of Abdul Baqua, whose life illustrates the many rags-to-riches stories in Dharavi, you get a bird's-eye view of Dharavi. You can see the maidan where the Western India Tanneries once stood. It is now used as a cricket ground by local children and for holding political meetings by local politicians. But this open space will be gone before long because the builders who have bought it will soon construct another high-rise like Vaibhav.

From Diamond Apartments you can see how Dharavi has been redeveloped only around its periphery while its heart remains untouched. For instance, on the outer edges of Dharavi, particularly along 60 Feet Road and the Sion-Mahim link road, you see buildings constructed under the Prime Minister's Grant Project in the 1980s, and the more recent Slum Redevelopment Scheme. There are also older private buildings like the Baliga Society in front of Diamond Apartments. And in the distance are the Nagri Apartments, also private, built on land vacated by the Shafi Tanneries.

The high-rises are still only eruptions on a low-rise, unplanned landscape of scores of settlements with distinct names and personalities. These settlements converge and part in mysterious ways. Where one nagar ends and another begins only the residents can tell you. And by what logic these divisions take place is also beyond the ken of the outsider.

The major part of Dharavi remains an area, like most other large slums in Mumbai, badly in need of organization, of sanitation, of adequate and clean water, and of decent housing. Large tracts of it also remain 'illegal', newly built settlements housing people who have moved out of the more settled areas, recovered their investment, and decided to start over in the hope of being 'settled' again. Given the past record, most such illegal settlements become legal over time. So the risk is not really as great as would appear on the surface.

An explosive mix

Dharavi represents the spirit of Mumbai and its cosmopolitanism. If you visit Dharavi, you might get the impression that the settlement is dominated by just Tamilians and Uttar Pradesh Muslims. In fact, the place is a real mix of many different communities. A survey in 1986 found that more than one-third of the people living in Dharavi were from Tamil Nadu. Of these, more than half are from just one district, Tirunelvelli. The rest of the population consists of people from Maharashtra, including the Kolis, from Gujarat, like the Kumbhars, from Andhra Pradesh, Karnataka and Kerala, and from Uttar Pradesh—specially Azamgarh and Jaunpur districts. There are also a growing number of people from Bihar and Orissa.

For years, Hindus from the south and Muslims from the north lived cordially with Maharashtrians. The clashes were intra-community and not inter-community. All that changed in the 1992-93 communal riots which tore asunder old friendships, divided on religious lines even regional groups like the Tamilians, erected physical barriers in settlements where Hindus and Muslims had lived together for decades, and created a permanent atmosphere of fear in the minds of the many who had lived through the worst. Says Mariam Rashid, a respected social worker with the Society for Human and Environmental Development (SHED), 'Even today, I rush out of my house if I hear a noise, or someone shouting, and think back to the days of the riots.'

Since those riots, a process of ghettoization has occurred. In some respects, communities of migrants tend to live together. It is a natural and accepted phenomenon. Thus, you might walk into one lane off the Dharavi Main Road and find that every single house belongs to someone from Jaunpur in Uttar Pradesh. And if you went to Kamaraj Nagar, off the Mahim-Sion link road, every family is from Tirunelvelli district.

But earlier there were many mixed neighbourhoods. After the riots, this is where you began to see the change in Dharavi. If Muslims were a minority in a Hindu settlement, they would move out, and if Hindus were a minority in a Muslim neighbourhood, they would move out.

Take Naya Chawl in Palwadi, for instance. In 1993, after the first spell of rioting in Mumbai, many walls were erected in Dharavi. Some were in the mind, others were in fact. One such wall, of brick and cement, came up overnight in the seventy-year-old Naya Chawl. This chawl is typical of some of the older constructions that still survive in Dharavi. They consist of a narrow structure, with a tiled roof, and single rooms all opening out in one direction. Two such buildings, each with eleven rooms, are separated by a small open drain. All the rooms have cemented front porches.

These twenty-two rooms at one end of this long structure are called Naya Chawl, Palwadi. All the residents of these rooms are from Tamil Nadu, many are in white-collar jobs in the railways, or are employees of multinational companies.

At the end of these eleven houses, you enter a narrower lane. All the rooms here have lofts and even balconies. They have encroached on the open space between the two sides, leaving only enough room for a few people to walk. As a result, there is no natural light and the chawl looks congested. The contrast between these two in some ways illustrates the differences between communities that have coexisted for generations. The crowded end of this lane is called Nawab Nagar. Practically all the eighty-nine families living in this part are Muslims. Their only access to the road is through Naya Chawl.

During the riots, a brick and cement wall was built at the end of Naya Chawl and the beginning of Nawab Nagar. Only a narrow gap, just enough for a single individual to pass, was left. The Tamils of Naya Chawl claimed this had to be done as they had been attacked by the Muslims. The Muslims of Nawab Nagar insisted that the attack on Naya Chawl was the work of 'outsiders' and that the wall was a gross inconvenience as it virtually blocked their access to the outside.

Six months after the riots ended, the wall came down. Not because the Naya Chawl Tamils wanted it but because the Muslims got the municipality to act on their behalf. The result of this obvious statement of the numerical majority of the Muslims is that Tamil Hindus from Naya Chawl have been moving out since the last six years. By mid-1999, nine of the twenty-two houses had Muslim residents. Like their kin in Nawab Nagar, the new residents of Naya Chawl have built a second floor and balconies. Before long, the difference between Naya Chawl and Nawab Nagar could disappear just as the name—imposed by the municipality—has become a common one.

But the story of Naya Chawl does not represent all of Dharavi. It continues to be home to distinct communities from north, south, east and west, many of whom live together, irrespective of caste or religion. Amina's part of Muslim Nagar, for instance, is a typical mix of communities speaking different languages, having different faiths, but supporting each other in their daily battle for survival.

Survival of the fittest

I have attempted to present Dharavi through the lives of the individuals who inhabit its lanes. I have focused on a few individuals to remind us that a slum is not a chaotic collection of structures; it is a dynamic collection of individuals who have figured out how to survive in the most adverse of circumstances. At the same time, although it is tempting to romanticize and valorize these individuals, we cannot forget that there is nothing to celebrate about living in a cramped 150 sq.ft house with no natural light or ventilation, without running water or sanitation. No one should have to live in such conditions.

The journey through the history and geography of Dharavi is essentially a journey into understanding how cities grow. Thus, the first chapter traces the growth of Dharavi and places it within the development of Mumbai, from seven islands to a megalopolis of over 12 million people. Patterns of migration, industrialization, land use patterns, the attitude of the State, the role of the wealthy, the survival tactics of the poor, the role of politics and politicians—all these are interwoven into the growth of Mumbai and, within that context, of Dharavi.

Not all the slums in Mumbai are like Dharavi. Although many slums are a mixture of communities and religious groups, there are few places like Dharavi in Mumbai which have such an amazing mix of people. Chapter Two looks at some of the different groups from various parts of India who have made Dharavi their home. Each has a skill, or a specific role that it plays in the life of the settlement. While some live separately, in pockets within larger settlements, others have intermingled and are spread throughout Dharavi.

What marks Dharavi from other slums is also its productivity. It is more like an industrial estate than a slum, except that people live and work in the same place. Chapter Three recounts some of the enterprises in Dharavi, how they were established, what they manufacture and in what conditions they operate. These are far from ideal conditions. All the worst sins of production in unregulated developing countries can be found here—sweatshops, hazardous industries, insanitary work conditions, exploitatively low wages. But at the same time, almost everyone seems to be employed in some kind of work. And many thousands have prospered through a mixture of hard work, some luck and a great deal of ingenuity.

Crime and slums are inextricably linked in the minds of most people. Are slum-dwellers criminals, or do all criminals live in slums? Has crime in cities increased because of the growth of slums and the illegality that surrounds them? Chapter Four looks at issues of policing a place like Dharavi, the problems that it poses and the kind of solutions that have been worked out by people living there.

And, finally, we look at the central issue, that of housing for the urban poor in Chapter Five. This is at the root of the emergence of a place like Dharavi. If the State and industry, which have fuelled the growth of Mumbai, had planned adequately for low-cost housing for migrant workers, some of the present crisis that the city faces would have been averted. Instead, the government's policy has been incremental and ad hoc. When pushed to the wall, some schemes are put in place, implemented half-heartedly, and abandoned at the first obstacle.

The problem with this approach is magnified today, given the sheer number of the urban poor. They are a crucial vote-bank. No political party can afford to ignore them. Thus, successive governments devise schemes to keep them happy, temporarily. But the long-term issue of affordable housing for the poor is rarely tackled. The result of such an approach is evident in a place like Dharavi, which is pock-marked with the debris of incomplete development schemes.

Dharavi, in fact, symbolizes the problem that growing cities in most developing countries face—that of unequal development. The countryside is deprived, stagnant; the cities become the 'engines of growth', attracting capital, creating avenues for work, providing access to services and allowing some people to make millions and many more to subsist. Inevitably, those who cannot survive in the countryside—usually the poorest—have no option but to migrate to the nearest urban centre.

What do you do with these rural migrants who arrive in cities with such regularity? Do you try to stop them from entering? That may be possible in totalitarian regimes but would be unacceptable in a democracy. Do you try and push them or persuade them to go back? This has been tried but in the absence of robust investment outside urban areas, such a reverse flow is unlikely and probably unrealistic. Even the plan of developing counter-magnets to big cities, the smaller towns, has not reduced the extent of rural migration to big cities. Indeed, urban growth in India suggests that the larger cities will continue to draw people even if smaller towns are also fulfilling the needs of the rural poor seeking employment.

The most recent government data (1999) reveals that one-third of the country's population, that is 71 million people, live in India's metropolitan cities (million plus) of which there were 23 in 1991 and are projected to go up to 40 by 2001. While India's population has increased two and a half times since Independence, its urban population has grown five times. An estimated 305 million people, or 30 per cent of the country's population, live in urban India, the second-largest urban population, after China, in the world.

Cities are not just growing; the number of poor people living in them is also increasing. One-third of urban dwellers live below the poverty line. These people are not just income poor but suffer deprivation in many other ways. For instance, 15 per cent of them do not have access to safe drinking water and half do not have adequate sanitary facilities.

There was a time when it was seriously argued that efforts should not be made to ease the lives of the urban poor by providing them basic urban services or housing, because then many more of their kin would rush to the city. Fortunately, better sense prevailed in the 1980s and this antediluvian mentality was discarded for a more realistic approach towards the growing number of the poor and homeless living in cities.

A place like Dharavi poses several difficult challenges for the government: should it be left alone, developed or pulled down and redeveloped? Should the State recognize its 'industrial' nature and provide it with facilities that will, at the very least, make working conditions for thousands of workers safer and cleaner? Or will doing that kill these enterprises? There are no easy, or obvious, answers.

This book does not try to answer all the questions about the future of the urban poor. It is merely an attempt to present another reality of our cities, one that we have to comprehend before solutions can be found. Without such an understanding, even the most well-intentioned efforts prove to be unworkable.

1

What is this 'Dharavi'?

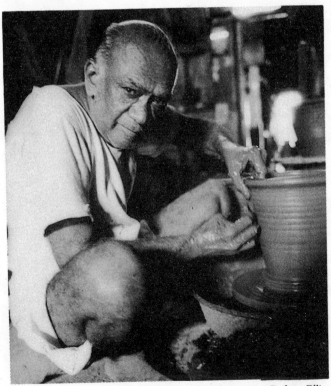

Rafeeq Ellias

'What is this Dharavi you are talking about?' an old man dressed in white kurta and dhoti and sitting on a *charpai*, asks me. 'Where you are sitting is Dharavi,' I counter. 'No,' he asserts as he takes another puff on his hookah, 'you are wrong. This is Matunga Labour Camp, not Dharavi.'

The elderly man responded the way many people do when you ask them about Dharavi. For, like Matunga Labour Camp, which is a settlement dominated by Valmikis, Dalits from Haryana who settled in Bombay over fifty years ago, Dharavi is a composite of many distinct settlements. Each has marked characteristics of the origins of its residents.

The elderly Valmiki's comment, in fact, tells the real story of Dharavi, of urban migration, where large slum settlements are created not by design, but by accident, and sometimes, as in the case of Dharavi, by benign neglect. For a place like Dharavi, the slum, is the creation of the city government, of sociologists, of social workers, of people who do not live in this connected and disconnected world of contiguous settlements.

His words remind us that places like Dharavi are stamped with the character of their different communities and trades—some of these live together, some, like Valmikis, live separately. But the majority relate to their own particular area. It is others who mesh these separate entities together into one 'slum'.

Dharavi could have remained a small koliwada, a fishing village on the banks of the Mithi river, had many different events not coalesced leading to the creation of 'Asia's largest slum'.

The first was the very process of the emergence of Bombay from seven islands and fishing hamlets to a city. The genesis of the port city of Bombay, as we know it today, began with the arrival of the Portuguese in India in the late fifteenth century and their capture of what they then called Bom Bahia (the Good Bay) in 1534. Despite its location and natural harbour, Bombay gained importance much later, after it passed to the British crown in 1661 as part of the dowry of the Portuguese princess, Catherine of Braganza, who married Charles II.

Things changed very little for Bombay despite this transfer of ownership. Bombay consisted of seven islands separated by low 'flats' that would fill up during high tide. The islands were inhabited by fisherfolk and agriculturists. In 1668, it was transferred to the East India Company. This marked the beginning of the development of the port which had been overshadowed greatly by the growth and development of Surat to its north.

Through the eighteenth century there were incremental changes in the city, but the speed of development accelerated in 1858 when Bombay reverted to the British crown. During this period, partly by design and partly by default, the land between the islands began to get filled up and there emerged a long island that tapered off to the south.

Gillian Tindall, in her book on Bombay *City of Gold*, describes how the local coconut tree was partly responsible for the reclamation of the land between Bombay's seven islands. She writes:

> Long ago, before the British or the Portuguese before them came, the palms were the main vegetation of the islands, and by a constant shedding of their great leaves into the shallow sea they gradually surrounded themselves with layers of decayed vegetable matter into which their roots could in turn burrow further . . . Central London is built on a terrace of river gravel, New York on rock, Leningrad on a marsh, Calcutta—notoriously—on the shifting black mud of a tidal estuary, but Bombay can claim the eccentric distinction of being largely based on rotten fish and leaves of the coconut palm.

Through the nineteenth century, Bombay's development as an important commercial and financial centre grew exponentially. The first textile mill in Bombay was established in 1854. Within two decades there were fifteen such mills and seventy by the end of the nineteenth century. As urban historian Mariam Dossal writes in an essay, 'Signatures in Space: Land Use in Colonial Bombay' in the book, *Bombay, Metaphor for Modern India*:

By the 1870s, Bombay counted among the colonial cities of significance within the British Empire. What had been a conglomeration of fishing villages and agricultural hamlets in the 17th Century, had grown into a port town in the 18th and a port-city of consequence in the 19th Century.

In addition to the natural process of reclamation, the British launched extensive reclamation works that linked the islands into one long tapering island city. Even today the island city is just 78 sq.km, while the suburbs that are part of Greater Mumbai make up the remaining 360 sq.km. The Mumbai Metropolitan Region, which extends further inland on the mainland, covers an area of 4,375 sq.km. But the distinct character of the city still obtains from the island city.

Unequal development

More than the geographical process that led to the creation of one island out of seven and the historical factors associated with colonial expansion that made Bombay an important port and commercial city, what is relevant in the context of what the city is today are two factors: one is the manner in which colonial cities traditionally organized themselves and second, the policies of subsequent city governments after Independence towards land use and housing, particularly for the working class and the poor.

Under colonial rule, the best facilities were reserved for those areas where the British lived. These included the southern part of the island and areas like Malabar Hill and Cumballa Hill, which offered residents a salubrious green location with a view of the Arabian Sea. By way of contrast, the native town extending north and east of these locations remained unplanned and poorly serviced.

These dominant characteristics have continued to mark the difference between different parts of the island city even today although the days of swamps and lack of sewerage are history. Mariam Dossal writes of how, in the late eighteenth century, the English had moved from south Bombay, where they initially lived, to what were then the outlying suburbs of Parel, Lalbaug, Byculla and Malabar Hill.

> Their desire for larger dwellings in healthier surrounding was shared by wealthy Indian merchants such as the Wadias, Camas, and Jeejeebhoys. The Fort area increasingly came to be used as a business district. In the Indian quarter, residential and work spaces continued to be mixed, with cluster patterns frequently following occupational and caste lines. (*Bombay: Metaphor for Modern India*)

Even today some of these divisions that date back to the eighteenth century continue. Thus, you find that Malabar Hill is still one of the most cosseted areas and best supplied in terms of basic urban services. The Raj Bhavan, home of the Governor of Maharashtra, occupies the best location in Malabar Hill while ministers of the state government live in Raj-style bungalows in an environment far removed from the rest of the city. There is never any water shortage in Malabar Hill.

But go to the localities of Girgaum, Khetwadi or Dhobi Talao, which were a part of the old native town, and even today they are crowded with a mixture of residential buildings and businesses. The water supply is intermittent and inadequate, the building stock is old and crumbling, drains are overflowing, garbage remains uncollected and the streets are too narrow to be broadened, thereby leading to overcrowding and unhealthy living conditions.

Thus, the inequalities that defined Bombay as a colonial port town have continued in some respects with little being done to set these right. Investment is always available to beautify the already well-endowed parts of the city. But there is no money to provide even basic services to the poorer areas.

The basic inequity in infrastructure becomes even more acute when one considers the needs of the poorest residents of the city living on unserviced, vacant, often low-lying and perennially waterlogged plots of land. Even if the government desires to give them basic services, such as water and sanitation, it cannot because the infrastructure does not exist. And the infrastructure will not be put in place because the settlement is deemed 'illegal'—a classic catch-22 situation.

How the poor live

Before Independence, a city known for its flourishing textile industry made some basic provisions for workers.

Thus, the well-known Bombay Development Department (BDD) chawls were built in Worli to accommodate the mill workers. These were three- or four-storeyed buildings with one-room tenements, each about 100 sq.ft with common toilets and bathrooms. Although more people lived in one room than had been envisaged when the chawls were built, for many decades they provided a roof over the heads of textile workers.

Similarly, the Bombay Improvement Trust (BIT) built chawls closer to the docks for dock workers and municipal workers. The BIT chawls in Imamwada in the heart of Mumbai's Bhendi Bazar area are today coveted accommodation compared with the more dilapidated buildings in the area. Chawls were also built for the police. In 1921, an estimated 70 per cent of the workers lived in these chawls.

Private builders also constructed similar chawl-like structures in Parel and the mill area for workers. Often more than one family shared a single room as the workers brought their wives and children from the villages. These buildings are still in use and they continue to be overcrowded. Although many of them are dilapidated and badly in need of repairs, they are much in demand in a city facing an almost insurmountable housing problem.

In a study of sanitation in India, published in the journal *Environment and Urbanization*, Susan E. Chaplin says the fear of the British that certain diseases would spread from the working classes to the elite neighbourhoods was one of the major motivating factors that prompted the city governments in Britain to undertake housing for the poor and the working class. But in India, the British were under no such compulsion although the plague in 1896 resulted in a flurry of activity with the setting up of the City Improvement Trust (CIT). It was asked to widen roads and improve housing conditions. The CIT also developed what were then the northern suburbs of the city—Dadar, Wadala, Matunga and Sion. Even today, evidence of these improvement measures exists in residential colonies that are well laid out with adequate open spaces. This is in sharp contrast to other parts of the city which did not benefit from any planning. These suburban residential colonies, however, were for better-off Indians while the working class had to depend on private and public chawls.

After this initial attempt to house workers, nothing more was done. After Independence, the better-serviced areas of the city continued to be occupied by the middle and upper classes. Unlike in the nineteenth century, when the fear of disease moved the British to undertake some improvements, there were no such threats to move the new ruling classes into ensuring equity in the distribution of basic services in the city.

With the expansion of industry in the city and its surrounding areas, workers were left with no option but to live in informal housing, in slums on vacant lands as the chawls were already overcrowded. What these workers were doing was not very different from their counterparts in the British industrial cities of Manchester and Birmingham, where textile mills spun and wove Indian grown cotton in the heyday of colonial rule. There too, workers were 'slumming' on the banks of the rivers close to which the mills were located. That was one of the origins of the word 'slum' denoting informal, unhygienic housing.

If the city had seriously wanted to plan for workers' housing, it would have been possible in the initial years after Independence. There was plenty of vacant land. The government could have made it incumbent on industry to provide housing for its permanent staff. A few enlightened industrial houses did this but the majority ignored this basic responsibility towards their workforce.

Instead, land owned by the municipality or the government was 'reserved' for various public facilities like parks, or schools, or clinics but was never actually used. And private owners, with vast tracts of land, allowed them to remain vacant in the hope that land prices would escalate and bring them larger profits.

The combination of vacant land and thousands of people with jobs but with nowhere to live led to the inevitable. Over time, many of these plots, particularly in the island city, became slums. Those who did not find vacant land squatted on the pavements, or along the railway tracks. A city with no plan for working class housing chose first to ignore this phenomenon. When it could not ignore it any longer, it proceeded to push people off the pavements and the vacant plots with the combined might of the municipal corporation's 'demolition squad' and the police.

Demolishing the poor

Inevitably, the demolition policy was pursued most vigorously in south Bombay from the 1950s onwards and large groups of people were relocated on the periphery of the city. Sandeep Pendse describes this process in his essay in *Bombay, Metaphor for Modern India*:

> Toilers are relegated to the periphery of existence in the city, both literally and figuratively; actually and ideologically. Areas occupied by toilers may be located on the periphery of the city. They may be found near the municipal boundaries of the city or in the extended suburbs. Toilers typically occupy the least developed and the least desirable land in the city. Slums, which have come to be the characteristic residential areas of toilers since the specially built chawls can hold only a fraction of the working class, originally occupied the newly reclaimed, low lying areas which joined the islands which today are united to form the city of Bombay. These landfills are prone to waterlogging and flooding. Later slums were located on undeveloped outlying patches of land or vacant spots within the city. When unpaid labour develops these areas and makes the localities habitable, increasing their market value, urban development plans are invoked to 'relocate' the slum-dwellers to new, undeveloped areas.

The Kumbhars of Mumbai illustrate this policy through the moves they have had to make in one lifetime. They came from Saurashtra to Bombay in 1877 when their region was ravaged by drought and set up their kilns in an area in south Bombay. But as the city grew, and with it the needs of the elite who lived in the southern part of the city, the Kumbhars had to be pushed further north. So they were packed off to Sion, on the northern edge of the island city. But once again the land on which they set up shop was needed—for a British army camp. So they were relocated, this time to the edge of the island city, close to a swamp that is Dharavi today. Thus, in fifty years this community has had to move three times, once from its original home to Bombay and thenceforth within the city.

A more recent example, which is singed into the memory of every slum-dweller, is the demolition of Janata Colony in Mankhurd in north-east Mumbai. This slum colony had come up in the 1960s on vacant land next to the Bhabha Atomic Research Centre (BARC) which extends from Chembur to Trombay. Its residents were pavement dwellers who had been moved out of south Mumbai and their kin who joined them as part of the stream of migrants constantly entering the city. Janata Colony had become a settled slum, with temples, mosques, churches and schools.

On 17 May 1976, at the height of the State of Emergency declared by the then Prime Minister, Indira Gandhi, 12,000 policemen entered Janata Colony and overnight threw out a community of 70,000 people. They were shifted four kilometres away, to a swampy area in Trombay which has now emerged as a large slum named Cheetah Camp. The demolition took place to free land to house BARC personnel—3,000 of them.

One of those who bore the brunt of police lathis in those days was a young slum-dweller from Karnataka, A. Jockin. The experience made him determined not just to fight for the rights of his kin but also to organize slum-dwellers so that they would be better equipped to negotiate with the State for their rights. Thus emerged the National Slum Dwellers' Federation (NSDF) which now has branches in thirty-four cities and a membership of around 12 lakh.

More realistic

The policy of demolitions finally yielded to a slightly more realistic approach towards slums in 1971. The Maharashtra Slum Areas Improvement, Clearance and Redevelopment Act was passed which empowered the government to improve existing slums by giving them basic services like water, toilets, drains, paved pathways and street lights. The law defines a slum in terms of structures and amenities. It does not look at the question of ownership of the land on which a slum is located. In other words, even if the government 'improves' a slum, the slum-dwellers have no legal right to continue living there.

Although the law spoke of redevelopment and improvement, in fact the government continued to concentrate on clearance. Under the law, all that the government had to do was to declare a slum unfit for habitation and it could demolish it. Thus, with one hand it 'improved' slums, and with the other it demolished them.

Conversely, those slums not declared unfit had to be recognized, improved or redeveloped. For this purpose, the Maharashtra Slum Improvement Board was set up in 1973. But its powers were limited to providing facilities, such as taps, toilets and electrical connections to slums located on government or municipal lands. More than half the slum colonies at that time existed on privately owned land.

A break with past policies occurred when the government decided to conduct a slum census in 1976 to gain a more accurate idea of the numbers living in slums. Slum-dwellers who could prove that they had been living in the same spot before 1975 would be issued a 'photopass', an identity card. Their slum would be 'recognized' and granted certain facilities. However, there would be no guarantee that their slum could not be demolished at any time if the government so chose. Still, this represented a major shift from the earlier approach, as reflected in the Bombay Development Plan of 1967, when the municipal corporation had hoped it would be able to clear all slums.

In 1976, the Urban Land Ceiling Regulation Act was passed. Its aim was to take surplus land in the hands of private owners and use it for public good. But as with many other such laws, the intention did not translate itself into action. Only a fraction of the land which the government could have taken with the powers of this new law was actually acquired. And the litany of 'no land' for poor people continued for decades thereafter.

In 1981, despite policies that seemed to suggest a more realistic and humane attitude towards the urban poor, another spell of demolitions was conducted. As if to remind all slum-dwellers of the might of the State, the municipal corporation and the state government embarked on another massive demolition drive at the height of the monsoon. Memories of the demolition of Janata Colony were still alive in people's minds. Thousands of pavement dwellers were thrown out on the streets, their fragile shelters ruthlessly torn down, their belongings smashed. Worse still, they were piled into buses and taken outside the city limits and told to 'go back' to the places from where they had come.

The crassness and inhumanity of this action raised an outcry amongst some sections of Bombay's residents who had, for the first time, become conscious about human rights after twenty months of the Emergency which ended in March 1977. A public-spirited journalist filed a writ petition in the Supreme Court arguing that these people were citizens of the country with the same rights as everyone else and could not be denied the right to life in this manner. By not providing them alternative accommodation, the State was denying them the right to life because they could not work if they had nowhere to live.

The case dragged on for four years and is now a part of the annals of history. But the 1985 Supreme Court judgement was a landmark in many ways because the court acknowledged that 'the eviction of a person from a pavement or slum will inevitably lead to the deprivation of his means of livelihood . . . and consequently to the deprivation of life'. Thus, if people could establish that they had lived in Bombay before 1976, the State would have to give them alternative accommodation in the event of a demolition. Furthermore, the State had to give them adequate notice before a demolition.

The judgement did not, however, solve the problem of the future of the slum-dwellers, for it upheld the right of the State to demolish slums. Moreover, the 1976 slum census had ignored thousands of people living on pavements and alongside railway tracks. These people were even more vulnerable because their status continued to be 'illegal' and they could be evicted without any guarantee of alternative accommodation.

It was the intervention of non-governmental organizations like Society for Promotion of Area Resource Centres (SPARC) and the Nirmala Niketan College of Social Work which recorded the existence of these communities. For the first time, a more accurate picture began to emerge of the people who lived on pavements and in railway slums.

The non-governmental census in 1985 pegged the number of pavement dwellers at 1,25,000. A couple of years later, another such census established that 18,000 households lived along the railway tracks. (At the end of 1999, there were an estimated 28,000 families living on railway land while the population of pavement dwellers had grown to around 3,00,000.)

The official census, despite its obvious shortcomings, was useful for one reason. It cleared up several false impressions about Mumbai. For instance, the Shiv Sena, which had emerged on the scene a decade before this census, had built its base in the city by arguing that Mumbai (at that time still Bombay), capital of Maharashtra, was being taken over by floods of non-Marathi speaking migrants, particularly from the south. The slum census established that of the 2.8 million people living in 1,680 slum settlements, the majority came from different districts in Maharashtra.

Officially, the government acknowledges that there are almost 5 million people living in slums, on pavements or along the railway tracks, that is half the population of Greater Mumbai. This great mass of humanity occupies only 8 per cent of the total land area of the city with densities going up to 18,000 persons per square kilometre. These numbers emphasize that the slum issue cannot be wished away, that it will not disappear if slums are systematically demolished and that it cannot be tackled as a side concern. Instead, it needs to be the central concern of city planners.

Improving slums

A decisive shift in the attitude towards slums came about only in the mid-1980s as a reflection of a worldwide reassessment of the role of cities in poor countries. In previous decades, the 'pull' factor of cities was seen as a problem which had to be deflected by developing the countryside and thereby negating the lure of cities. By the 1980s it was clear that the poor who came into cities were not just gainfully employed but provided essential services which cities needed. An informal census of Dharavi, for instance, revealed that only 10 per cent of the people were unemployed. In the absence of a welfare system, none of them were living off the State. Thus, they provided for themselves and for the city through their labour.

The change in attitude towards the urban poor in Mumbai also coincided with the realization that many of the swampy and useless plots of land which the poor occupied had now become centrally located, valuable urban property. As Jockin likes to put it, the poor are used as bulldozers to fill swamps, even out the land, make it habitable and just after this happens, the city moves in and they are moved out—to another uninhabitable plot of land.

Yet, even if the poor found work, the majority lived in great poverty. According to a 1985 survey, 80 per cent of slum-dwellers and 90 per cent of those living on pavements earned less that Rs 600 per month. Economist Madhura Swaminathan has argued in an article in *Environment and Urbanization* that poverty amongst the urban poor should be measured not just by looking at income levels but at other measures, such as access to safe water, sanitation and nutrition levels. She argues, 'While the incidence of income poverty, using official norms and data from the National Sample Survey, is lower in Bombay than in other urban areas of India, there is no doubt that in respect of incomes and consumer expenditures, on an average, people who are homeless or live in huts or tenements are substantially worse off than the rest of the population.'

Swaminathan illustrates this by quoting from a survey of notified slums in Bombay undertaken in 1981 which revealed that there were on an average 203 users for every tap in a slum settlement and that in some, the number went up to 8,600. The situation with toilets was worse. There were no toilets in 174 slum settlements out of the 619 surveyed by the Census of India in 1981.

And according to the National Commission on Urbanization, quoted by Swaminathan,

85 per cent of children up to the age of six in urban slums in India are malnourished. In our survey of children under the age of five in a Bombay slum in 1993, 61 per cent of boys and 72 per cent of girls were malnourished on the basis of a weight-for-age index.

The very nature of slum formation, which consists of incremental growth over land which could have multiple owners, tripped up the government's new schemes—slum improvement and, later, slum upgradation. The entitlements under these schemes were applicable only to those slum-dwellers whose names appeared in the 1976 slum census. Later, 1980 was fixed as the cut-off date after another slum census was conducted. And as the census only looked at huts on municipal or state government land, it created logistical problems within slums. For instance, there were slums where pockets of private land were located within larger tracts of government-owned lands. The huts on these private plots were not included in the census and were thus not eligible for the benefits. The government's programme involved paving the lanes between huts, or providing street lighting. How could this be implemented in such situations? Inevitably, even the little that could be done for slums was not done because of such complications.

In a large area like Dharavi, this complication was even more apparent. Even after the census, Dharavi continued to sprout 'illegal' settlements. These come up even today, on any unguarded vacant land or on land 'accidentally' reclaimed from the Mahim creek. Such land belongs to no one as it did not exist when the government made plans for the slum. As a result, no one knows how to deal with such areas.

Illegal slums

An example of this kind of illegality in the midst of areas that have now become legal can be seen even today in Dharavi. Across the Mahim creek, which is now a big open public toilet used by men, is one of the worst settlements in Dharavi—Naik Nagar. Next to it is the smaller Ambedkar Nagar. These areas are a reminder of what Dharavi was like thirty years ago.

You enter Ambedkar Nagar through a slushy and dirty approach road past the public toilet which reeks of neglect. Before you is the picture of urban blight at its worst. The road is not paved and is slushy from water overflowing from public toilets. Stones have been placed in puddles to allow people to access the settlement from the main road. This is an area that has grown in the last ten or twelve years. It is an illegal, unrecognized settlement. Therefore, it is not entitled to any of the benefits that the government offers through its slum improvement and slum upgradation schemes.

Halfway down the approach road, at a small paan-bidi shop, sits a man with an almost luminous face. He is from Orissa, he says. His son runs the shop. He has lived in Dharavi for thirty-five years in another 'legal' settlement. Why did he move here? 'My other son already had a sweetshop at the top of the road,' he says. But why court illegality? Because in Dharavi everything illegal becomes legal in due course, he says. Thus, Ambedkar Nagar lives in the hope that soon it too will be recognized.

And to help it in the process is Ashfaq Khan, social worker he claims, politician we know. In fact, like the budding politicians you find in all slums, Ashfaq has an unerring instinct when it comes to detecting a journalist. He zooms in on me as I stand at the paan-bidi shop. This young man, in his thirties and a resident of Ambedkar Nagar, is already sporting the attire of politicians, white kurta and pyjama and a mobile phone. He promptly gives me all his contact numbers.

Within minutes, the show is on. Ashfaq, the impresario, summons men and women as they cross us, prompting people to tell their stories, filling in details that they might overlook. He stops Gorappa, an

impressive elderly man in a dhoti and kurta with a
Gandhi cap on his head who is on his way back from
work and prompts him to talk about himself. Gorappa
is from Belgaum district, mends umbrellas once the
rains lash out, and repairs tin trunks and dabbas (lunch
boxes) at other times. He wanders around the city with
his bag of tools doing odd jobs. Like the man from
Orissa, Gorappa too lives in the hope that 'something'
will be done to make life in Ambedkar Nagar a little
more bearable.

All these people call their settlement Garib Basti
because almost everyone is poor and is doing odd jobs.
Unlike other parts of Dharavi, you will not find
workshops here. Yet, even Ambedkar Nagar yields
surprises. For even here you come across people holding
permanent jobs. Santaraj from Gulbarga, Karnataka,
works with the Central Railway. Why does he not live
in railway quarters? 'Because almost 30 per cent of my
wages are cut to pay for the rent,' he says. 'That's why
people like me prefer to live here.'

Others have moved here by selling their photopass
in a 'recognized' settlement elsewhere in Dharavi. This
is the only way they can generate capital for eventualities
like the marriage of a daughter or illness of a family
member. They are prepared to suffer the inconvenience
of living in a place like Ambedkar Nagar for a while.
They are used to this. In time, this too shall pass, they
hope, and eventually all of them will have a photopass
by the grace of Ashfaq Khan or some other politician.
'You need around Rs 12,000 to "buy" a photopass',
says Gorappa. 'No one has that kind of money in

Ambedkar Nagar. *Yeh to hai garib log ka basti.*'

Even more illegal than areas like Ambedkar Nagar are those that come up on accidentally reclaimed land along the Mahim creek. For instance, at the tail-end of 1999, Dharavi came into the news yet again because a fire devastated 4,500 huts. The majority of them had come up within the year on a plot of land which was a part of the Mahim creek until it emerged as almost solid land, the result of illegal dumping of construction debris. No one bothered to check. People in the neighbourhood saw the pitches coming up. The houses were made of wood and tarpaulin. It required little effort to set the whole area on fire. Even with a name like Rajiv Nagar, there was no respite for this community living on the edges of Dharavi.

These areas, the legal and amidst them the so-called illegal, illustrate the complexities of slum improvement or redevelopment.

The genesis of Dharavi

According to Jockin, the genesis of a place like Dharavi lies in the policy of demolition and relocation that the city followed for many years. Many communities that were moved out of areas in south Mumbai like Kamathipura, Tardeo, Reay Road and Khetwadi or Sonapur were pushed to what was then the edge of the city, Dharavi. What they found was swampy, unhygienic surroundings. The only solid ground was at the edges of the swamp, or where there had been accidental reclamation through the dumping of garbage and construction debris.

Jockin recalls that in the 1950s and 1960s, Dharavi was a favourite dumping site because it was closer than the designated dump at Deonar, which is much further north. Contractors found they could make more trips if they emptied their loads in Dharavi rather than going all the way to Deonar. In the lackadaisical manner in which such operations work even today in the city, no one cared, least of all the authorities. And over time, as if on its own, large parts of the swamp got filled up. After that it took no time for people to occupy this veritable no-man's land. But even this constant dumping did not change the swamp-like nature of Dharavi until much later.

Some of the early residents of Dharavi recall that when they entered the area from Mahim station, they had to build an access path themselves as there was no road. People placed rocks on the marshy ground, covered it with mud, and created a dirt road. As there was no electricity, they had to carry lanterns after dark. Today, that same dirt road has become Dharavi Main Road, a potholed, ostensibly tarmac 'main' road.

While some communities have had to move several times as the city grew, those who found themselves in Dharavi did not have to move again. The reasons for this are very special. Dharavi has emerged in a triangular strip that comes in no one's way, as a former urban development secretary of the Maharashtra government, D.T. Joseph, pointed out. To its west is the Western Railway with Matunga and Mahim stations. To its east is the Central Railway and Sion station. And to its north is the Mithi river. This triangle of different settlements which gradually merged into one large conglomeration is what is called Dharavi today. Its location ensured that the land was not needed for any other purpose. As a result, the people who came to live there—by choice or because they were forced to do so—did not have to move.

Another reason, argues Joseph, for people remaining in Dharavi is because it provided work. He points out that town planning, since colonial days, has been in the hands of engineers and architects who have not bothered about employment. The reality, however, is that people live where they can find work.

The 'pull' factor

Dharavi's story is not very different from that of other slums but it varies in some crucial respects. It is similar in that it developed as an illegal informal settlement barring the Koliwada, which already existed, the Kumbharwada, which was a planned relocation, and the Matunga Labour Camp. The rest were settlements that developed over time. As the politics of slums changed, parts of Dharavi were 'recognized' piecemeal and 'regularized'.

But what sets Dharavi apart from other slums is its special 'pull' factor. This was one of the areas which early on in its existence was recognized as a manufacturing centre. It was home to the tanneries because of its proximity to the abattoir in Bandra. Later, during the prohibition years, illicit liquor

Ayesha Taleyarkhan

Cutting edge: While there are a couple of garment exporters, there are many garment manufacturers who cater to the local market.

distillation became big business. The tanneries were asked to move out in the 1980s when the abattoir was moved to Deonar. Although the bigger ones did move out, the smaller ones continue even today. But the illicit liquor business continued right up to the mid-1980s.

The leather tanning business was replaced by a flourishing leather finished goods industry, garments and literally hundreds of other manufacturing units of all sizes. Dharavi was one area where any new migrant could find work. In fact, surveys have established that while in other slums, less than 10-15 per cent of people living in them work there, in Dharavi it is the other way round.

In the last four decades, the migration patterns in

Dharavi have followed the contours of the composition of the early settlers. Thus, tanners from Tirunelvelli ensured that more of their kin came to Dharavi. And the tanners of Azamgarh in UP did likewise. North and south met in the leather industry. More potters came into Kumbharwada, this time from Junagadh. The Valmikis from Haryana living in the Matunga Labour Camp were joined by many more from their villages when they heard that there was regular work available in the municipal corporation's conservancy department. The latest wave of migrants has been from Bihar, of young boys who work as unpaid apprentices in the leather finished goods business or in garments. In every community you hear stories of success. It is rare to find so many such stories concentrated in one area.

Dharavi drew workers who were self-employed in the informal sector industries that spawned in different parts of the settlement, as well as workers from the formal sector who were not provided housing. In many settlements, even today, you find blue-collar workers from well-known multinational companies, from the railways, the municipal corporation, the police, as well as thousands of former textile workers who lost their jobs after the 1982 mill strike and the subsequent closure of many of Mumbai's oldest textile mills. Workers who had land in their villages, particularly in the Konkan, could go back. But many workers from other parts of India who had worked in the mills had nothing to go back to. So they stayed on, and found other jobs.

Men like David from Jajapur in Mehboobnagar district, Andhra Pradesh, who came to Dharavi in 1955.

His father used to sell herbal medicine. David found a job in Kohinoor mills in the ring frame department where he earned around Rs 150 a month. By the time he left in 1982, when the mill closed, he was earning around Rs 700 a month. Now he works on construction sites, or wherever he can get some work.

Seated in his dimly-lit 6 foot by 8 foot room in Dharavi's Subhash Nagar, just off 90 Feet Road, this dark, small-built former textile worker speaks with immense sadness of the fate that has befallen him and others like him with the virtual demise of Mumbai's once-flourishing textile mills. 'Many like me have gone to the village. I used to have land in my village but not any more. We have learned to adjust where we are. Now my wife sells bananas. My daughter works in a tape cassette shop, another works in Kala Killa and one is in school,' David tells me.

'We have been living here since 1958,' says David. 'At first, our house was made of chatai. Slowly we managed to improve it by putting half-brick walls and tin sheets. The municipality paved the lane in front and built a drain.' One of the walls stands out as it is the only one fully made out of bricks. This is because David's neighbour has managed to make his home pucca. But in all these years, David has been unable to accumulate enough money to improve his house. In contrast, some of his neighbours have managed to make their houses pucca, using bricks and cement, and have built lofts that have doubled their living space. When I ask him what he feels about this, David merely shrugs. That simple gesture says it all.

The changing face

The face of Dharavi has changed dramatically in the decade from 1989 to 1999. Other large slums have also benefited from the government's slum upgradation policies and the slum-dwellers' individual efforts to improve their dwellings. But the change in Dharavi has been much more noticeable. Indeed, it underlines again the misnomer of referring to the area as a 'slum'. Parts of it are still slum-like—because they are still illegal—but much of Dharavi today is a settled area where people have either got place in high-rise buildings that have been constructed under various government schemes, or have devised ways to improve their own dwellings.

The relocation of larger tanneries in the 1980s freed up land which private builders utilized to construct better quality high-rise buildings than those constructed under government schemes. As a result, the new rich of Dharavi have not had to move away from their place of work—and the place that gave them their riches—but have continued to live there. Former tanneries like the Western India Tanneries and Gold Filled Leather now sport such buildings on their land.

Housing for the urban poor and the emergence of slum colonies are inextricably linked. As D.T. Joseph points out, the absence of any planning for housing for workers in industrialized areas inevitably results in informal housing settlements. But by their very nature and location, they make the possibility of replacing them with formal housing additionally difficult. He says, 'Ultimately, in any urban set-up, it is the people who are living there who count. And what do they want? They want a job, a place to live in, and some basic social requirements like a school, a shop or a hospital. That, according to me, is urban development. To my mind, you don't have a policy anywhere which covers this area.'

Dharavi, like other slums or slum-like areas, is an inescapable reality in Mumbai. There are practically no areas in the city where you can avoid the sight of a slum because the urban poor, or people forced to live in informal settlements, are half the city's population. The engineering approach to this problem has been tried and not worked—clear land of slums, push slum-dwellers out of sight, and expect that life will go on. The purely architectural approach has not worked either—where you plan for a well-designed settlement that will be pleasing to the eyes of the elite but will be dysfunctional for the people who need to live there. Thus, for instance, in Dharavi there were plans to free space for parks. But who would decide which households had to be moved?

As Joseph emphasizes, town planning has been elitist because it failed to understand the employment needs of the poor. He blames the elitism of town planning concepts, that continued to determine the attitude of the city towards slums, for the problems that Mumbai faces today.

Jane Jacobs, in her seminal work *The Death and Life of Great American Cities*, had a lot to say about the misplaced attitudes of urban planners that Mumbai's planners should note. Even if the context within which she wrote about slums was different—in American cities, slums were inner-city areas that got depopulated and neglected—her words have a contemporary resonance:

> Conventional planning approaches to slums and slum-dwellers are thoroughly paternalistic. The trouble with paternalists is that they want to make impossibly profound changes, and they choose impossibly superficial means for doing so. To overcome slums, we must regard slum-dwellers as people capable of understanding and acting upon their own self-interests, which they certainly are. We need to discern, respect and build upon the forces for regeneration in real cities. This is far from trying to patronise people into a better life, and it is far from what is done today.

The men and women who live in the incredibly crowded lanes and bylanes of Dharavi and other Mumbai slums certainly know what they want. They have survived without any assistance from the State. Some of them have devised solutions to their problems that are realistic and workable. Now that assistance is being offered, it should not stifle the spirit of enterprise that so dominates urban settlements like Dharavi. Instead, it should build on it. Unfortunately, the basic attitude of the State remains paternalistic—of a father doling out favours to children who do not know what is best for them.

2

Allah ka Gaon

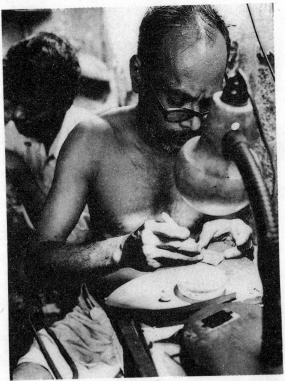

Rafeeq Ellias

This is one of the years when Bakri Id and Mahavir Jayanti coincide. Dharavi has a festive air about it. Everyone is dressed in new clothes. The girls have on their best jewellery. Khatija is wearing a white embroidered sari and is showing off her gold jewellery. Her daughter-in-law, who can only speak a few words of Urdu, is laden with gold and wears a bright red salwar kameez, befitting a new bride. Bowls of delicious sheer korma are brought out immediately on our arrival.

Sixty-seven-year-old Khatija is a handsome woman, tall by Indian standards. Her hair has turned red with henna; she jokes that she is growing younger each year. Khatija came to Mumbai from Kasargode in Kerala after her marriage when she was merely fifteen. Her husband used to work in a hotel in Dadar. When he lost his job, they were forced to move out of their rooms above the hotel. That is when they came to Dharavi, in 1961, and were given temporary accommodation by their *jaatwallahs* in the Malabar Sangam.

Describing her early years in Dharavi, Khatija recalls, 'First there were a few scattered *jhopdas* here and there. Then the dadas entered the picture and they built several huts and began selling them. They took over the land. There was an *aurat* dada who is still alive. She does *ladki log ka business*. Before I came here, Lakshmi dada was here. Which year? I can't remember but it was the year they introduced the "German" (meaning aluminium) 10 paisa coin. But I do know that I've been in this house for thirty-eight years, right here in Dargah Chawl, Social Nagar, Dharavi.'

Khatija typifies a resident of this city. She speaks with theatrical, exaggerated gestures. Describing how she had to literally fight for survival in the past, she says, 'In those days it was open theatre, full, *ao maarna hai to maro.*' Her language is pure Bambaiya. It has the crudeness yet directness that characterizes Mumbai's lingua franca, a mixture of Hindi, Urdu, Marathi, English and any other language you might fancy. At times she gets fed up of living in Dharavi, she admits. But, she says, 'See Mumbai is not like our *desh*. Here people from fifty villages have come to live. It is *allah ka gaon.*'

Women like Khatija represent just one of the myriad communities that reside in mixed settlements like Dharavi's Dargah Chawl. Most of Dharavi comprises places like Dargah Chawl where there is a mixture of Hindus, Muslims and other religious groups, people from north and south. Some areas, however, are inhabited predominantly by one community. Thus, there are enclaves which are entirely Tamil, others with people only from Uttar Pradesh, and still others where the Kolis live. But, as Khatija says, Dharavi is a village made up of people from more than fifty other villages; it is literally a mini-India.

The Dharavi mix, if one can call it that, emphasizes a central facet of Mumbai which we tend to forget in an era of identity politics, that this is a city of migrants. These are the people who have given Mumbai its distinctive culture, a mix of many different cultures from north and south, east and west. It is where Bambaiya, popularized by Hindi films but spoken every day on Mumbai's streets, comes from. It is the attitude, the energy that has come to signify the commercial centre of India.

From the very beginning, it was the possibility of employment that drew migrants to Bombay. Early migrants came from Maharashtra, particularly the Konkan, to work in Bombay's textile mills. By the mid-nineteenth century more people had begun coming in from north and south India for specific trades. But the majority of migrants then, as today, continued to be from Maharashtra.

Between 1941 and 1951, the population of Greater Bombay grew by 76 per cent, partly because of the influx of people into the city following Partition. It continued to grow thereafter for the next three decades at an average of 40 per cent. This finally slowed down in 1981-91 to just 8 per cent, placing the population of Greater Bombay at 9.9 million. A major reason for this was the shifting out of manufacturing units from the island city. As a result, the attraction of finding work in the formal sector diminished dramatically.

At the same time, the northern and eastern edges of the city grew exponentially. These were the places where new industries came up in the belt extending from Thane to Panvel and beyond. Not surprisingly, most of the new informal settlements were located closer to these areas of work.

Unlike these newer slums, Dharavi came into existence not only because workers did not have housing. It grew from a fishing village that already existed. Its early inhabitants comprised displaced communities from other parts of the city. Next, despite its insanitary environs, people came to live here because they found work in Dharavi and not in an adjoining neighbourhood. And, finally, Dharavi became what it is because the nature of the work determined the kind of migrants that came to live there. Thus, the early migrants were from Tamil Nadu and Uttar Pradesh, consisting mostly of men who came to work in the tanneries, and Kumbhars from Saurashtra, who came to join the potters already living there. Later waves of migrants found work in the leather finished goods business—including Maharashtrian leather workers—and in the garment industry.

Ayesha Taleyarkhan

The final gloss: Finished leather goods have taken over as the main leather-based business in Dharavi.

A survey of Dharavi conducted in 1986 revealed that Tamilians constituted one-third of the population, closely followed by people from Maharashtra. Other states represented were Uttar Pradesh, Karnataka, Andhra

Pradesh, Gujarat, Kerala, Rajasthan and Bihar. These figures would have altered only marginally in the last fifteen years with an increase in migrants from the north, specially Bihar. But there have not been any recent surveys to establish precisely how much the profile of the population has changed.

The caste profile of Dharavi is also linked to the nature of work. It is dominated by scheduled castes from different regions, the majority of whom work in leather-related activities, ranging from treating raw hides to crafting finished goods from processed leather.

As people lived where they worked, inevitably Dharavi developed with enclaves that were exclusively inhabited by people from a particular region. Over time, the select nature of these settlements has altered. Yet there are still several settlements where almost everyone comes from a particular district. As a result, you have a 'duplicate' Tirunelvelli district in one part, where only Tamil is spoken, or a 'duplicate' Jaunpur district, or Gonda district of Uttar Pradesh in another part. People living in such enclaves tend to be more isolated, do not mix socially with other groups, and keep to themselves. Those living in these separate settlements also include the Kumbhars from Saurashtra, the Valmikis from Haryana, and the Nadars and Adi Dravidas from Tamil Nadu.

Even within larger mixed settlements, there are sections which are dominated by a particular community. Thus, you find in one section of Transit Camp, built to accommodate those displaced when Dharavi's 90 Feet Road was widened, a community of the Konchikoris, a group of itinerant magicians and performers, who came originally from Solapur. Today, apart from moneylending, they make brooms.

The Valmikis from Haryana mostly work either as municipal sweepers or as sweepers in private buildings. Their settlement, which is a part of the Matunga Labour Camp, is a replica of a village in Haryana. You see women, their heads covered, cooking on open stoves, goats tethered to the side and men sitting on a *khatiya* smoking a hookah.

Kumbharwada, where a community of potters from Gujarat has lived since 1932, has a distinct personality of its own. All the houses accommodate the potter's wheel and a bunch of houses open out into an open space where there is a shared kiln for firing the pots. Over time, the Kumbhars have developed their own social links and keep to themselves. There are few cases of inter-marriage between Kumbhars and other communities. They have their own way of settling disputes and only turn to the police if this does not work. And they have evolved a cooperative system of buying commonly needed supplies like cotton waste for lighting their kilns. Thus, the Prajapati Sahakari Utpadan Mandal serves many different purposes: it buys cotton waste, it runs two rationing shops, a bal mandir (a creche) and a clinic.

What is common to all these groups is that they came to Bombay because of dire economic need. They were economic and environmental refugees. The first Tamilians, for instance, came to work in the tanneries of Dharavi because they could not survive in Tirunelvelli. Small farmers were wiped out after years of drought. Similarly, the first Kumbhars came to Bombay after a drought in Saurashtra. The Muslims from Uttar Pradesh also came to work in the tanneries as they could find little work in their districts of Jaunpur and Azamgarh.

Under these circumstances, the communities tend to stick together, to help their own kind. Thus, when people from Tirunelvelli set up tanneries, they went back to their district to find workers. The Uttar Pradesh Muslims did the same. Over time it is these two communities that grew in numbers as leather was the main business in Dharavi.

Barring nomadic groups like Konchikoris or the Gondhali Samaj who are from Karnataka, most other groups maintain strong links with their native place and visit their village every year, funds permitting. In May, almost every other house in Dharavi will be locked as its occupants will have gone to their village.

Many recent migrants to the city invest not just in their own property but in community resources in their native place. Such a link is particularly evident among the Tamilians from Tirunelvelli. Yet, despite these links, most of the people you speak to, regardless of whether they are from the north or the south, identify Mumbai as their home.

However, men and women are likely to have a different perspective. For men, Dharavi provides work and sustenance. For women, it means living in cramped surroundings, lack of privacy, difficulties of water and sanitation, and often carrying a triple burden of work. They work in their homes and also have to take up not just one but often two jobs. As a result, women like Kamala, a Valmiki, says, 'Compared to this place, our

Ayesha Taleyarkhan

Gruelling work: Hides are brought to Dharavi and unloaded for processing; the annual turnover in the raw leather business is estimated to be around Rs 60 crore.

village in Haryana is so nice and clean. Even though we don't have toilets, we can go in the fields. Here it was dirty earlier and it is still bad. Our young people don't have any work. People keep contact with their villages. We have a house in our village but we have kept it locked.' She hopes some day that she will be able to go back.

No going back

The only people for whom the question of going back anywhere does not arise are the Dharavi Kolis. They believe Dharavi belongs to them. And indeed it does. Dharavi, the fishing village, existed long before Dharavi, the slum. In the *Gazetteer of Bombay City and Island*

Vol. I (originally printed in 1909, published by the Executive Editor and Secretary, Gazetteer Department, Government of Maharashtra, Bombay), Dharavi finds mention as one of 'six great Koliwadas of Bombay— Mazagaon, Varli, Parel, Sion, Dharavi and Bombay.' According to this record,

> In 1727, Bombay consisted of two towns, Bombay and Mahim and 8 villages, Mazagaon, Varli, Parel, Vadala, Naigam, Matunga, Dharavi and Colaba. It had 7 hamlets, two under Vadala, two under Dharavi, and three under Parel. It had five Koli quarters and three salt pans.

The Dharavi Koliwada is located at the north-end of Dharavi Main Road. One end is marked by a cross, dated 1850, which is enclosed by a low fence. This, according to the *gaonpatil* (village head), Francis Patil, marks one of the oldest Koli settlements in Mumbai. Patil's house, an impressive two-storey structure, is opposite the cross.

Among the Koli families living in Dharavi today, 80 per cent are descendants of the original Kolis. Francis Patil, for instance, became gaonpatil in 1992. But his family has held this title for over eighty years for seven generations. The gaonpatil is common to both Hindu and Christian Kolis.

Till 1964, several families amongst the Kolis still made a living out of fishing. One of them was Kisan Killekar. He says that the fish from Dharavi was the best, the crab was particularly famous. Dharavi Kolis would supply shellfish to all of Mumbai.

The fishing stopped mainly on account of the

pollution in the Mahim creek. The fish would smell of kerosene. The fishermen blame the factories upstream in Chembur which, they allege, were discharging untreated effluents into the stream. Such fish could not be sold. As a result, even the few who continued to make a living out of fishing had to stop.

The Dharavi Kolis had a unique style of fishing. They would take on lease fishing rights which allowed them to build a dam across the creek. At high tide, the fish would enter and would then be trapped in the dammed section. At low tide, fishermen would wade into the water with nets and catch the fish live. This kind of fishing is not done anywhere else in Maharashtra, claims Kisan Killekar.

Killekar lives in a house which is over seventy years old. It gives you an idea of what Koliwada would have been like before shops encroached on the road that leads through the settlement and thus hid houses like Killekar's. It consists of a main room with a high ceiling and a wooden balcony loft covering a third of the room. Several rooms lead off from this main room. A poster hanging from the loft shows that Killekar and his wife, Teresa, who was a Shiv Sena municipal councillor, used to perform Koli dances. The house still has its original tiled roof.

Today, Killekar is a bitter man. Until 1964, his family had managed to make a living from fishing. But with continuous land reclamation, particularly along the Mahim-Bandra stretch, the sea receded. And with this the unique creek fishing of the Dharavi Kolis also died. While the communities living near the open sea, such as those in the Mahim Koliwada, can still survive on fishing, inland communities like the Kolis of Dharavi had to find other avenues for survival.

From fish to alcohol—an unlikely transition, perhaps, but a natural one for many Kolis. For brewing alcohol is a Koli tradition as much as fishing. 'Even today, many Koli families make their own country liquor,' says Killekar. They brew the liquor in their homes, using in the preparation a wide assortment of fruits—jamun, guava, orange, sweet lime, chikoo and apple. The fruits are allowed to ferment, then the fermented liquid is heated and distilled crudely. The resulting brew is potent and popular.

The Dharavi Koliwada 'country' was famous in all of Mumbai. The reason for this was twofold, according to Ramakrishna Keni, a local Shiv Sena politician. One was a suitable environment. Dharavi had open spaces, it had marshland where barrels of country liquor could be buried to ferment. Then, it had salt water which was the speciality of the liquor brewed there. The Kolis' life revolved around two things, says Keni, *mahasagar* and *navsagar* (the ocean and liquor).

Prohibition, imposed in 1954 when Morarji Desai was the chief minister of Bombay province, did not stop the Kolis. They called Desai's rule *country-bandi* and not *daru-bandi*, saying that he was only interested in stopping country liquor and not all liquor. 'We had a system,' says Keni. 'Why should we be coy about it? We had "managed" the police. All the police stations were informed about our vehicles and these were never stopped. We shared our profit with the police, so no one suffered. We used to make four trips a day to Bombay to supply country liquor.'

Even today, the Dharavi Kolis claim that no one else knows their formula for making country liquor. 'While the Kolis of Versova and Worli added sweet water to their brew, ours was with salt water,' says Keni. 'We had our own society which started with seven members and grew up to between twenty and thirty members. We stored the liquor in wooden vats and when it was ready, transferred it either to tin boxes (usually used for oil) or to tyre tubes. The latter were favoured because people could carry these around their necks, it was easier to walk through the swamp with your hands free, they could take up to thirty litres in two tubes, and in the dark, the tube could not be easily spotted.'

The Kolis continue to live in Koliwada and are today only 6 per cent of the total population of Dharavi. They maintain the system of having a gaonpatil and are a close-knit community with an almost equal number of Hindus and Christians. But the younger generation is moving out, to other jobs and other locations. Thus, Koliwada will inevitably have to face changes as their *gaon* also changes.

Duplicate Tirunelvelli

Trains from south India coming to Mumbai terminate at the Kurla terminus or in Dadar. Only a few go all the way to VT (Victoria Terminus) or CST (Chhatrapati Shivaji Terminus)—the beautiful Gothic structure that remains VT to most people despite being victim to the rampant name-changing disease which has resulted in Bombay becoming Mumbai and VT being rechristened CST. A sizeable number of those who alight from these long-distance trains go directly to Dharavi, where there are entire settlements inhabited by people from Tirunelvelli district.

Kamaraj Nagar, off the main Mahim-Sion link road, is like a small village from Tirunelvelli district recreated in Mumbai. It is spotlessly clean. Each house has a little sit-out decorated with rangoli. Torans hang on the doors. The children are bright-eyed and curious. Many men wear the traditional Tamilian dhotis. The only language you hear is Tamil. Most of the women speak only Tamil and are cautious about talking to strangers. But their children speak English.

Even if you did not know that one-third of the population of Dharavi is from Tamil Nadu, you would guess it if you took a walk down Dharavi Main Road from the Koliwada end. You will see shop signs in Tamil. The jewellery shops in particular make sure that their boards are in Tamil. Even at the other end of the road, where there is a concentration of Muslims from Uttar Pradesh, many shops display Tamil signs. The owners of these shops are aware that just around the corner is one of the oldest Tamil settlements of Dharavi—that of the Adi Dravidas living around the Ganesh Mandir. The temple is the oldest such structure in Dharavi, dating back to 1913.

Amongst the Tamils of Dharavi, there are three main communities. The most populous are the Adi Dravidas, who are scheduled castes from Tirunelvelli district. Next come the Nadars, who used to be toddy tappers but thanks to the famous Nadar leader and Congressman K. Kamaraj, the community got educated and has progressed. And the third section of Tamils are the Thevars, an OBC community from Ramnathpuram.

The Adi Dravidas were mainly small and marginal farmers. Many of them came to Dharavi and found work in the tanneries alongside Tamil Muslims from the same and adjoining districts. Today, with the closure of tanneries, and higher levels of education, many of them have managed to find work in the railways, in textile mills, or hold white-collar jobs.

Education is highly valued amongst all the Tamil castes in Dharavi. They proudly tell you that they are also educating their girls, even though lately this has led to the problem of there not being enough educated boys to marry these girls. The Tamil children can attend one of the four municipal-run Tamil schools, which are only up to Standard VIII. Thereafter, they have the option of either joining the Kamaraj High School, a private institution which is English-medium, or some other school outside Dharavi. In the past, Tamil children would be sent back to Tirunelvelli to study either in a boarding school, of which there are several, or to stay with members of their extended families back in the village.

The office of the Adi Dravida Samaj is located on Dharavi Cross Road, a muddy lane that connects Dharavi Main Road and 90 Feet Road. It is a long, narrow room decorated with a variety of Ganesh calendars. A portrait of Dr Ambedkar is prominently displayed at one end. Tamil magazines hang on a string along one wall; they are available for members who come to the office for a reason, or even without a reason.

Across the office is a large compound, measuring 12,500 sq.m, which belongs to the Samaj and which accommodates the Ganesh Mandir and sixty-four Adi Dravida families from Tirunelvelli. The temple, an important landmark in Dharavi, originally consisted of a small shrine under a peepul tree. According to the local priest, the Ganesh idol was brought from Varanasi in 1913 and installed in this spot. The building around it was only constructed in 1939 and the rest, which consists of a *navagraha* used for weddings and other ceremonial occasions, in 1992.

The Adi Dravida Samaj is active in community matters. In the past, one of its important members was S.K. Ramaswamy, a municipal councillor. SKR, as he was called, had apparently fallen out with the infamous Tamil ganglord, Vardarajan Mudaliar. But ask any of the Adi Dravidas if SKR had any connection with Varda or whether he had been involved with the liquor business and they vehemently deny any connection. 'All that might have been true before SKR got married,' says a leading Adi Dravida. 'But why do you want to rake up the past in your book?'

Whatever the truth, it is clear that SKR was a name to contend with in Dharavi, with a loyal following among the Adi Dravidas. When he stood for the municipal elections in 1985 from the Dalit Muslim Mahasangh, the party started by well-known smuggler Haji Mastaan, he won by a huge margin. His nearest rival from the Congress lost his deposit. SKR, according to Selvaraj, made his money through the scrap business, mainly plastic. So much money, in fact, that he could afford an apartment in one of Dharavi's first high-rise buildings, Diamond Apartments. His son lives in that apartment today.

According to the Adi Dravidas, SKR would hold court in the Samaj office. Members of the community would come to him with all manner of complaints and problems and he would settle them. 'He never asked for money from people. They paid him on their own,' claims Selvaraj. SKR died following a heart attack while on a visit to his home state of Tamil Nadu in 1987.

Today, the man who calls SKR his *saga bhai* is seventy-two-year-old P.N. Selvaraj Mehta from Tirunelvelli. He is an intriguing and articulate character. The surname Mehta, which is completely non-Tamil, derives from the fact that Selvaraj worked as an accountant in a tannery as he was one of the few educated people in those days. As accountants were generally knows as Mehtas, Selvaraj took that as his last name.

Selvaraj's story is, in many ways, similar to that of other Tamilians living in Dharavi. His father's uncle came to Dharavi in the early 1900s, before the Ganesh temple was built. His father had also worked in a tannery but later began trading in leather. The eldest in a family of fifteen brothers and sisters, Selvaraj was born in his village in Tamil Nadu while the rest were born in Dharavi. He studied in a Tamil school in Dharavi up to Standard IV and was then sent back to the village to study up to Standard X. After completing his education, Selvaraj was recruited to work in the tanneries.

Unlike Selvaraj, K.M. Perumal, who is also an Adi Dravida, came to Bombay at a later date, in 1951. He came thinking he would get work and lived initially in a 'Pongal' house. This living arrangement, unique to

Dharavi, continues to survive in a changing city. Pongal houses are huts in which anywhere between thirty and hundred men sleep. A survey conducted in 1986 identified sixty-two such Pongal houses in Dharavi. In those days, men like Perumal paid about Rs 8 per month to live in a Pongal house. This amount guaranteed them a space on which they could unroll their mat and sleep. They bathed in the open; taps were located conveniently in front of these houses. For the price they paid, the men got a mat, on which they slept and, more important, two square meals a day, one with rice and the other with chapattis.

In 1961, Perumal got a job in the weaving department of Kohinoor Mills in Dadar where he worked until the 1982 textile strike. 'Thanks to Datta Samant the mill closed down and since then I have been out of work,' says this bitter sixty-one-year-old. Like other former textile workers, Perumal survives on odd jobs. There are thousands of textile workers in almost every community living in Dharavi. Some of them have been reduced to earning daily wages by working on construction sites.

Younger Adi Dravidas like Ashok Kumar have done better for themselves. Ashok today is one of only two or three people from his community who are still in the leather business. His father, K.A. Vaidvel Muthu, came from Tirunelvelli in 1933 and the family has lived in Dharavi ever since.

Ashok's father left his village because as a small farmer he could not survive. He came to Bombay looking for work and found it in the tanneries which were run by Muslims from Tirunelvelli. Tannery owners would go to Tirunelvelli to recruit workers. On a starting salary of Rs 5 per day, Ashok's father began working in Dharavi. Today, Ashok owns his own business. In one generation, the family has moved from poverty to prosperity, a story that is heard almost everywhere in Dharavi. 'For India, Mumbai is the Centre, for Mumbai, Dharavi is the Centre,' says Ashok, explaining why even people like him who have done well for themselves continue to retain their links with Dharavi.

The best-known Thevar in Dharavi is Muthu Thevar. You cannot miss him if you happen to enter Dharavi from the 60 Feet Road-end of Dharavi Main Road. One of the first sights you see is a mock fort. On most mornings, you might spot a swarthy, dark man, his shirt open up to his waist, numerous heavy gold chains gleaming against his hairy chest, sitting on the step of the 'fort'. On either side of him stand Sten gun-wielding guards. This is Muthu Thevar, the Shiv Sena shakha pramukh. He watches everyone entering Dharavi through the main road.

Walk past him into Kalyanwadi and you will see low-rise structures, even plantain trees. All this in the middle of Asia's largest slum? Yes, this is Kalyanwadi, another bit of Tamil Nadu transplanted in Mumbai. On the first floor of one of these houses is an air-conditioned wallpaper-covered cabin. Behind two glass-topped desks sit a man and a woman. Both are well known in Dharavi.

The man is called Krishna Seth. He is neither a Marwari nor a Gujarati as the name might suggest. He is a Thevar from Tirunelvelli district—Krishnan is his name. He became 'Seth' because he was one of the new breed of successful businessmen in Dharavi. He is a politician affiliated to the Congress and is also chairman of the Dharavi Slum Improvement Committee.

A young woman sits in the revolving chair next to Krishna Seth. Everyone knows and acknowledges her. She is S.P. Mary, or Paulene Mary, who won the 1992 assembly elections from Dharavi on a Congress ticket. She tried again in the next elections, as a candidate from a different party, but was defeated. Paulene is also from Tirunelvelli, but she is a Christian and a Nadar by caste.

The men who take us to meet Krishna and Paulene are Adi Dravidas. A Brahmin, who heads the South Indian Cooperative Bank, is also in the room. You have a mini-Tamil Nadu right here. 'We have no disputes amongst us,' they assure me, 'because here we are a minority.' The caste battles are saved up for Tamil Nadu. However, there is a little bit of collective amnesia here as Dharavi has seen caste battles between Tamil groups in the past.

As we talk, a dark man, a heavy gold chain around his neck, enters. He bears a strong resemblance to the Shiv Sena shakha pramukh Muthu Thevar. P.S. Pattan Thevar is Muthu's uncle. He says there are around 5,000 Thevar families in Dharavi. Most of them are in white-collar jobs. Asked how come his nephew joined the Shiv Sena despite the party's history of antipathy to south Indians and the riots in 1967 which many of these people remember, Thevar says, 'South Indians have turned to the Sena because they are not stressing on their being south Indians but instead saying that they are Hindus.'

Tamil politics in Dharavi follows patterns established

in the home state. Caste loyalties and political loyalties are clearly defined. Most of the community is educated, highly enterprising, involved in many different trades and businesses as well as in professional jobs. Increasingly, since 1992, large sections of the Tamils, regardless of their caste, are beginning to support the Bharatiya Janata Party. During the 1992-93 riots, some of the worst incidents of rioting involved the Tamils. The riots also divided the Tamil Muslims from the Tamil Hindus for the first time since the two groups migrated to Bombay and settled down in Dharavi.

Dharavi's Dalits

The majority of communities living in Dharavi, whether from the north or the south or from Maharashtra, are Dalits. Dharavi is a reserved scheduled caste constituency. One of the groups that bitterly complain about this are the Kolis, who feel they stand no chance of getting elected. Others tried to fudge their caste for the sake of winning elections and faced problems following their exposure.

One of the more distinctive Dalit communities are the Valmikis from Haryana who have lived for over half a century in Matunga Labour Camp. The men are less than forthcoming when I go and question them. The women, however, have no hesitation in talking to me.

Kamala is the wife of Karan Singh, the local Congress activist who is also a special executive magistrate. They live in a two-storey structure which looks far better appointed than the homes of their neighbours.

'I came to Bombay after I got married. Actually, I

was married at the age of eleven or twelve but came here seven years later. When I came, my husband was unemployed. We lived in this very spot in Dharavi and many of our neighbours also came before or during that time. Later, he got a job with the Boots company. But it closed down a few years ago,' says Kamala.

Like others of her community, Kamala, who has four girls and two boys, complains bitterly about the lack of opportunities. 'Most of our people get jobs as sweepers with the municipal corporation or work in buildings. The women also work in buildings,' she says. As many as 95 per cent of women and men work. Despite women's participation in wage labour, the community remains conservative in its attitude towards them. Kamala, however, has educated her daughters and is determined not to allow them to marry as young as she was married. 'I don't even remember when exactly I got married,' she says ruefully.

The Valmikis remain aloof from other communities. Kamala, for instance, admits that even though she has lived in Mumbai for so many years, she does not speak Marathi. 'We only know our own people,' she says.

Kamala's neighbour, Kesarbai, is also from Haryana. She is much older than Kamala and has lived in Dharavi for thirty-five years. 'I was nine when I got married and went to live in my mother-in-law's house. I came here when I was sixteen. There were very few women here. We were only three women in this chawl, while there were seven men in just one house. There was no electricity then. We used to light gas lamps and cook on kerosene or on our *chulhas*. We still make rotis on *chulhas* because our men will not eat rotis made on gas or on a kerosene stove,' she explains.

Kesarbai's neighbour is a Maharashtrian. Indubai Borade looks as if she is in her seventies but could well be younger. Like the other women around, she cannot tell her exact age. She is slightly bent, the result of years of sweeping and swabbing other people's homes. Every day she walks several kilometres to Dadar where she works as a domestic in three houses. At the end of the day, she trudges back to Dharavi. When I met her, she had just returned after a hard day's work and could barely stand.

Dressed in a typically Maharashtrian purple sari and with an impressive pearl *nath* on her nose, Indubai, from Beed district of Maharashtra, sits down on her doorstep and recounts her story. 'I got married and came to live here. I had one boy and four girls right here', she says pointing to her tiny 5 feet by 8 feet hut. 'We used to wash utensils in people's houses then, and even today we are doing that.' Like her sisters from Haryana, Indubai was married at the age of twelve. 'When I came here only people from the Valmiki Samaj lived here. Even though we are from different communities, there is no problem. My husband used to work in a grinding mill. We built this house ourselves. Earlier, there was no water. We had to spend all night getting water. There were long queues and there would often be fights. Sometimes, after waiting all evening, we would get water after midnight. There was also no electricity then. I can't remember how many years we managed to do without light. Now we have a tap. We get water for three or four hours a day though we still have to fill and store water.'

Indubai recalls that while the Maharashtrian women would go and fill water, the Valmikis would not allow their women to go out. The men would go and fetch water. The women still maintain purdah.

The Valmiki temple in Matunga Labour Camp, which is about fifty years old, was built through donations from the community. Says the pujari of the temple, 'Despite the fact that both my wife and I work and earn fairly well, we still don't get any respect from society. That's one big problem. Even if we educate our children, our caste people can't get jobs.'

An additional problem is establishing their caste status. I met Shrichand N. Dhika, the pradhan of the Valmiki Samaj, in a local public call office (PCO) run by another Valmiki. This elderly, white-haired man is from Delhi. He came to Dharavi fifty years ago and works for the municipal corporation. He says that when he came to Bombay around 1,500 people lived in the area and the atmosphere was good. 'Now lights have come but the dirt has also increased. First we had water, and it was clean. Now the population has grown, and even though we have toilets, they get full in just four days. There are too many people. There are more than 12,000 people in just Labour Camp. And even if there are more taps, there isn't enough water and there are always fights over it.'

Both he and the owner of the PCO, Lalchand Padwal, confirm that sometimes their people are forced to buy 'caste certificates' to establish that they belong to the scheduled caste and are thus entitled to the benefits guaranteed to them under the Constitution. Says Padwal,

'We have become refugees. If we go back to our state, they say you don't belong here. And here too it is only for Maharashtrians ever since the Shiv Sena government came to power. They demand proof of fifty years continuous stay.'

The men confirm that the rate for obtaining a caste certificate is Rs 3,000 to Rs 4,000. 'Sometimes we buy a false certificate and then get stuck. But without it, we can't do anything, can't get into college, can't stand for election,' says Padwal.

Dalit communities from Andhra Pradesh and Karnataka have also settled down in Dharavi. Unlike the Valmikis, many of them have managed to find jobs other than those of sweepers. Men like seventy-year-old Narasappa, who is from Imlapur in Karnataka's Gulbarga district, consider themselves lucky for having found a permanent job. He worked for years in the railways as a driver of a staff car. He lives in a municipal chawl near Subhash Nagar which is more than eighty years old.

Narasappa's father worked for twenty-eight years in the railway workshop in Parel. As a result, both Narasappa and his brothers managed to get jobs in the railways. Others from his community worked in the textile mills. But after the 1982 strike, many of them were rendered jobless. Now they do odd jobs and survive. As they didn't have anything in their villages, they could not go back and have had to continue living in Mumbai.

Roseamma is a programme supervisor with Community Outreach Programme, one of the oldest non-governmental organizations working in Dharavi.

She joined in 1977 as a community health worker after being trained in Sion hospital for a year. She also did a diploma in tailoring and trained as a Balwadi teacher. 'I took every opportunity to work,' she says.

Roseamma, a Christian, was also born in Imlapur like Narasappa. Her father, who worked in Mumbai, sent her to the village to get educated. She returned at the age of eighteen after getting married. Her husband is a guard in the railways. She has four sons.

The Andhra-Karnataka Dalit Varga Sangha was formed in 1975 in Mahim. Instead of spending money on an annual Ganpati celebration, they decided to collect money for a school. Today, the Ambedkar School, started in 1987, is an important English-medium school in Dharavi.

The adjacent locality of Subhash Nagar is like any village in one of the southern states. The children have just returned from school. A young boy is helping his mother roll papads. They are part of the Lijjat papad brigade in Dharavi who collect the premixed dough and get paid for rolling out and drying the papads.

Lilavati lives with her husband and two sons in a tiny 6 feet by 8 feet room with a half-loft. In this space they have a bed, a TV set, a radio, shining stainless steel vessels hung on one wall, and a gas stove near the door. Within minutes, she turns out delicious south Indian coffee.

Her sons sit on the floor while we sit on the bed. They have no hang-ups about where they live. The older boy, who is doing his B.Com. and wants to do computer science, says that he likes Dharavi because everything is so convenient.

What is striking about Lilavati and Narasappa is the absence of any self-pity at their situation. In Lilavati's case, this has clearly made a difference in her son's attitude towards being a resident of Dharavi. In his mind, living in Dharavi is like living anywhere else in Mumbai. It is not something to be ashamed of. He speaks in a matter-of-fact way about how he wants to learn computer science and had contemplated buying a computer but realized that there would be no place in the house to keep it. So, he says, he will wait till their area is redeveloped and they get a little more space.

The UP-wallahs

Just as Kamaraj Nagar is a mini-Tamil Nadu, there are enclaves in Dharavi that replicate particular districts in Uttar Pradesh. You realize this once you step off Dharavi Main Road and walk into a small settlement where only people from Jaunpur district reside.

Ayesha Taleyarkhan

Hides in plenty: The raw hides are first washed, salted and then treated further in the leather-processing godown.

Eklakh processes leather. He lives in an extended family. On both sides of his house, large by Dharavi standards, and across are friends and acquaintances from Jaunpur. One of them is Mohammad Yasin.

Why did his people come to Mumbai? Yasin says it is because jobs were easily available. So families that came would send a message to their villages, where large families had to survive on the yield of small plots and rainfed agriculture. 'In UP, all we had was poverty and politics,' he says.

They might have escaped the abject poverty of their villages by coming to Mumbai but they did not entirely escape the politics. 'I can remember the days when we used to play cricket with the Koli boys on Dharavi Main Road,' recalls Yasin. 'They would send us Diwali sweets, their women would come over here for Id to have sheer korma.' But 'ab to jamana badal gaya hai,' he says ruefully. 'The Shiv Sena has spread poison. Otherwise they were good people.'

Why and how has the distance grown between the two communities? Why was there harmony earlier?

Yasin believes that the harmony came from people doing the same kind of work. Hindus and Muslims worked together in the tanneries that dotted Dharavi. Earlier, these tanneries were owned by Englishmen. Just before Independence, Punjabi Muslims bought several tanneries from the English owners. But once Pakistan was established, many of these Muslims left. The ownership changed hands again but the new owners continued to employ Hindus and Muslims. Thus, unity was based on people being in a similar situation.

There was tension between Hindus and Muslims in 1947, at the time of Partition, recalls Yasin and then

again for a short while on the day Mahatma Gandhi
was assassinated in 1948. This fear and suspicion
continued till the early 1950s. But after that, right up to
1992 and the demolition of the Babri Masjid, there was
no fight between the Hindus and the Muslims living in
Dharavi, he says. In 1984, the Bhiwandi riots did have
some impact and the emergence of the Shiv Sena as a
force also contributed to the insecurity of the Muslims.

In numbers, the UP Muslims are fewer than the
Tamils and the Maharashtrians, but because they own
shops and businesses, their presence is visible in Dharavi.
The UP-wallahs continue to organize themselves
according to the district in UP from which they have
originally migrated. They are also divided according to
the religious sects to which they belong even though
they united against the Shiv Sena consequent to the
1992-93 riots.

Many of these divisions find their roots in intra-
religious differences that can be traced back to their
native districts. For instance, eight years after the Hindu-
Muslim riots of 1992-93 had united all the Muslims in
Dharavi and even determined their political loyalties—
a large number flocked to Mulayam Singh Yadav's
Samajwadi Party considering it the only party interested
in the Muslims—the community was divided between
the Berelvis and the Deobandhis over the control of the
Badi Masjid. So bitter is the dispute between the two
sides that there have even been instances of minor
rioting.

No fixed address

Apart from settled communities like the Tamilians,

people from Uttar Pradesh and different Dalit groups, Dharavi also has a few distinct nomadic groups who are identifiable because of their trade and lifestyle. Deep in the confusing bylanes of Muslim Nagar—one of the largest extended settlements in Dharavi—live members of the Gondhali Samaj. They live by their wits, yet they remain poor. Unlike the Kumbhars, they have no skill to sell. But they can sell just about anything.

In many parts of Mumbai, you often see women from this community, known as the *bartanwallis*. They carry a load of stainless steel pots and pans on their heads and go from house to house. If you have old clothes in reasonably good condition, they will buy the clothes off you in exchange for one or more stainless steel pots. There is much haggling and fighting in the process.

In the evening, these women return to Dharavi with their baskets full of clothes and the remaining pots. They make their way to their homes in Muslim Nagar and lay out the old clothes. Local merchants then come and inspect the clothes and buy them after several rounds of energetic bargaining. In the process, some of these women earn between Rs 50 and Rs 100 a day.

The community is originally from Gulbarga and many of them still speak Kannada. But they have lived in Mumbai for many years and have started speaking Marathi. Officially, they are deemed a nomadic tribe. However, they do not fall within the category of the scheduled tribes and have only recently been recognized as OBCs.

'But we get no benefit from this,' says Ashok Kashinath Vairal of the Bharatiya Vimukta Yuva Front, who is also part of the Gondhali Samaj. His tribe got its name because of the 'gondhali' ceremony that they perform on occasions like weddings and naming ceremonies. It consists of an invocation and devotional songs interspersed with small dance steps which the Gondhali perform. Members of the Gondhali Samaj are also fortune-tellers, people who do what is called the parrot trick whereby a caged parrot has been trained to pick up cards and tell the fortune of a person. Ashok estimates that there are around 4,000 families from his Samaj in Dharavi. There are an equal number living in Ambernath, an industrial area on the Mumbai-Kalyan highway.

The majority remain uneducated. Education of girls is particularly poor. As I speak to a group of women, they stare fascinated as I write down what they say. 'What are your problems?' I ask them. 'We earn through hard work and our men drink it away,' says one. 'What if you refuse to give them the money?' I ask. 'They beat us, that's what happens. In any case, in our community men can have two or even three wives, all living in the same house.' When that 'house' happens to be one small room, one can imagine the problems. If the first wife has only one child, and the second produces three, there are daily fights over food for the children. Life is not peaceful.

The Gondhali Samaj at least has a trade of some kind. One community that seems to be known only for breaking the peace are the Konchikoris. They are the moneylenders, the people who replaced the Pathans after Partition. The Konchikoris or Makadwalas are accused of charging a rapacious compound interest and using any means to collect their dues. As a result, they are feared and hated and stories about their tactics and lifestyles abound in many corners of Dharavi.

Seventy-six-year-old Vasant Siddharaj Shivpur speaks passionately about the plight of his community. Vasant came to Bombay with his family in 1942. There were fifteen or twenty families belonging to his community who came from Solapur. Some of them had monkeys. They also brought donkeys. The women would read palms, the men would hold monkey shows and all of them would make brooms and baskets to sell. That is how they lived.

When they first came to Bombay—travelling by train from Solapur without a ticket—they got off at Dadar station and headed for a rocky outcrop in south Wadala. Vasant can remember clambering over a fence to get to this spot. They survived by begging. There was a British military camp close by and a train carrying food for the troops would pass by. They would beg and somehow survived on the food they got from the British soldiers. Their houses were made of packing paper and bamboo sticks.

In 1944, when the land on which they lived was needed for another purpose, the Konchikoris were shifted to Dharavi, to an open space near what was then a textile mill, the Jasmin Mill. This was not far from Mahim station and the area was called Labour Camp.

In 1952 they moved again, closer to Kumbharwada. And then in 1984, when the authorities needed that land to widen the 90 Feet Road, they were moved again, to their current location in Transit Camp.

Earlier, there were many areas in Dharavi covered with grass. As a result, the Konchikoris found it easier to get the kind of grass they used to make brooms. Today, they have to travel as far as Palghar to get the *malli ullu* which they use.

Besides their traditional skills of being itinerant entertainers, or broom and basket makers, the Konchikoris have branched out into some new trades. At the time when country liquor brewing was flourishing in Dharavi, they would work as labourers in the stills, carrying tyres full of the liquor. They never had the capital to set up their own stills.

Now most of them have jobs as sweepers in the municipal corporation. Some work in the docks while others own taxis. But many have also made money through moneylending. According to the Valmikis, the Konchikori moneylenders charge a usurious interest. 'The Marwaris take 2 to 3 per cent a month but the Makadwalas charge 10 per cent a month,' says Lalchand Padwal, a Valmiki from Rajasthan. He says people give their photopass, which is a slum-dweller's most precious document, as security against loans from the Konchikoris. Often, people end up forfeiting these photopasses.

Despite the wealth some Konchikoris have accumulated through moneylending, Vasant complains, 'Even if they've managed to earn, they don't know how to use it. They have not invested the money in anything productive.' He despairs when he says, 'We haven't moved ahead because we have no education. Nobody listens. Our people don't know how to behave and we still continue to beg. Just because we have money, we can make people bend. But it doesn't earn us respect. Young people get mad at me when I say such things, but it's true.'

Vasant's own life is as colourful as that of his people. He was educated up to Standard III in Kannada. His first real job was as a crane operator in the docks, in New Dock No. 1 which had the mobile crane department. He worked there from 1957 to 1965. Why did he leave a secure job? Because he was caught stealing! 'We used to steal machine parts, fill them up in a truck and take them out. We would take care of the police and customs.' But the returns were poor and he ended up losing his job. A case was registered against him but nothing could be proved. Fortunately, by then Vasant had started driving a taxi in his spare time. When he lost his job as a crane operator, he bought two taxis and began his career as a taxi driver, an alternative job which did not last long.

Vasant was married when he was only ten years old to a girl of seven. 'She started going astray when she grew up. I couldn't explain anything to her, nor did I want to beat her or kill her,' he says, without a trace of remorse. So he let her go and at the age of twenty-eight got married again, to a woman who has been educated up to Standard IX and who is eleven years younger than him.

Of the three sons his first wife bore him, only the youngest survived. His second wife gave birth to a son, who died, and then to three girls. All his daughters are educated, says Vasant. The eldest is married and has eight children. She didn't have a son, so she kept trying, he says, by way of an explanation, and the youngest has four children.

'Our marriage custom is A-1,' Vasant says proudly. 'In the old days, the boy's family had to give the girl's family 12 gm of gold. But all that has stopped now. The only thing they give now is a *lugdi choli* (sari and blouse) to the girl's mother, a dhoti, kameez, *petha* (turban) and chaddar to the father, and a red sari, white blouse and bangles to the girl, as well as a mangalsutra which the husband ties around her neck. The couple are blessed by four people.'

Widow remarriage is accepted amongst the Konchikoris but it is not done with the same fanfare as a regular marriage, nor are marriageable age youngsters allowed to witness the ceremony as it is considered that this would bring them bad luck.

Unlike Vasant, Yellapa Shankar Konchikori has a steady job as a sepoy at the Shramik Vidyapeeth, one of several non-governmental organizations working in Dharavi. He is trying to bring about some changes in his community. Even though their names have been removed from the list of notified criminal tribes, he is angry that the police continue to treat them as criminals. 'Unemployment is a big problem among our youth,' says Yellapa. 'I joined Shramik Vidyapeeth in the hope that our youth would come forward. But barring a handful, they haven't responded.'

Yellapa, however, has managed to persuade some members of his community, three boys and a girl, Sumati Mane, to be trained as social workers. They want to create awareness about health issues in the community. Girls are rarely educated among the Konchikoris even today. Sumati, one of the first girls to be educated, stands out in the community not just for having completed her schooling but also for having continued to do social work after marriage. Sumati encourages other children in her community to complete their education; she earns by giving tuitions to children in the colony. She has made sure her own children are educated and wants her daughter to have a career.

Despite her education and the fact that three members of her family are working—while one brother works in a bank, another brother and father are insurance agents—Sumati lives in a tiny two-room *kholi* in the Transit Camp. Education has not brought them the surplus capital to be able to improve their living standards. Her family has not followed the new Konchikori occupation of moneylending. As a result, like many others in Dharavi, they are unable to build up savings which will enable them to either move out of where they live, or improve their small house. Sumati, however, does not grumble about the lack of space. 'I am used to it,' she says stoically. What vexes her immensely is the scarcity of water, which comes only for a few hours every day. Also, the toilets are dirty and some distance away. And during the rains, the narrow lane separating two rows of houses is like a river of sewage.

The four sections of the Transit Camp where the Konchikoris live are a hive of activity even as darkness sets in. In every home people are working, making brooms or baskets. Those who do not participate in this cottage industry purchase brooms from a factory which makes them and go out and sell them. Some of the children manage to make as much as Rs 50 a day selling brooms.

Inevitably, things will begin to change even in these communities. Young people like Sumati are getting educated and have aspirations that go beyond following the traditional trades. Even their conventional work of making brooms is being overtaken by machine-made brooms which are cheaper. There are problems finding raw material. All this will force the Konchikoris and the Gondhali Samaj, who are also bound to be affected sooner or later, to take on other occupations within another generation.

Will it last?

Apart from the groups described in this chapter, there are many more identities hiding in the settlements that comprise Dharavi. There is, for instance, a large group of people from Kerala—Hindus, Muslims and Christians. Recent waves of migrants have been dominated by people from Bihar. Most of those doing machine embroidery in badly lit rooms are from Bengal or Bangladesh. There are Marwari and Gujarati jewellers and Maharashtrians from various districts involved in different trades.

Despite this diversity, or perhaps because of it, Dharavi has been known to be generally peaceful compared to many other large slum settlements in Mumbai. The reason can only be the desire of the majority of people living there to get on with the job of earning their living. As Ramjibhai Pithabhai Patel puts it: 'We do our work. We are working people. We don't have time for anything else. We work from 7 a.m. to 7 p.m. If we don't work, we die.'

But how long will this last? For the identity politics of the 1990s has already divided people from the same region who worked in the same industry. Muslim and

Hindu tanners from Tamil Nadu were united because of their work. They considered themselves to be 'Madrasis'. Today, they identify themselves as Hindus or Muslims. The exceptions are too few to make a real difference.

Underlying the communal tensions are economic tensions. New waves of migrants are willing to work for a fraction of the wages of older workers. When these two are from two different regions of India, and also from two different religions—as in the case of leather workers where the new workers are Muslims from Bihar who are displacing older Maharashtrian Hindu or neo-Buddhist workers—then the ground is ripe for further communal strife.

Within each of these communities, the politics of their native states continues to exacerbate divisions. Thus, amongst Tamilians, the political alignments and realignments in Tamil Nadu find an echo in their ranks. The same goes for the UP Muslims. The Dalits, too, are divided into different factions of the Republican Party of India. No political party has succeeded in gaining an overwhelming foothold in Dharavi because of these multiple political configurations.

Apart from communal tensions and politics, there are other changes that are taking place. A generation that has grown up in Dharavi, of Adi Dravidas, Muslims, Kumbhars and other communities, is educated and has aspirations that go beyond the trades pursued by their fathers. These young people are in white-collar jobs and in time could move out of Dharavi to areas where their distinction would be lost.

Education is also creating social problems. For instance, both UP Muslims and Adi Dravidas complain that they cannot find suitable grooms for their highly educated girls. The Kumbhars insist that even if their daughters have to marry someone less educated than them, the boy must be from their community. So even Ramjibhai admits to having married off his highly educated daughter to a barely educated young man. The rumblings of change can already be heard in many of these communities.

The downside of this education spiral is that many young Dalits, in particular, are not finding jobs and also do not want to do the kind of work their parents are doing. The Valmikis complain bitterly about this. And amongst Muslims, although girls remain in school, boys still drop out and their mothers worry that they will get sucked into the world of crime.

In a sense, what is happening in Dharavi is not very different from the changes taking place in many small towns in India. The big city is forcing a breakdown of social and caste barriers yet politics is forcing communities into becoming more insular and conservative. The future will depend on how these diametrically opposite trends are reconciled.

3

Turning Scrap into Gold

Rafeeq Ellias

In 1948, an eighteen-year-old boy from Tirukoyoor, in Tamil Nadu's South Arcot district, travelled to the city of Bombay. He knew little about the city, or city life. But he bravely ventured forth as it was difficult to survive in his drought-hit village.

Shamsuddin thought he was coming to a big city. Instead, he found himself in a swamp—an area called Dharavi—where his uncle, Sheikh Hussain, lived. He had apparently lived in this swamp since 1914. Says Shamsuddin, 'I found work in my Mamu's business— rice smuggling. In those days, Bombay city's limits ended in Mahim, just west of where my Mamu and his sons lived.' Grain brought in from outside the city limits was taxed. But Hussain, his three sons and his newly arrived nephew had already worked out a way of getting around the system.

'Every day, my cousins and I would make several trips to distant Virar, then located outside Bombay, where we would buy rice for 1 rupee and 14 annas per pound. We would carry packets of it back as our personal belongings, get off at Mahim station, and walk through the *khadi* (swamp) to Kalyanwadi where Mamu lived. The rice would then be sold for Rs 10 per pound.'

Shamsuddin's uncle lived in Dharavi until 1954-55 and then went back to his village. His three sons decided to emigrate to Pakistan. As a result, the rice trade stopped. Shamsuddin had no money and no work.

He managed to find a job in a local coal company where he earned the royal sum of Rs 1.50 a day. After two years, his prospects improved when he got a better job at the Atlas Printing Press in Madanpura for Rs 56 a month. This gave him the confidence to get married, in 1959, to Hayatbi from Tambaram, Tamil Nadu. While his wife has never been to school, Shamsuddin has studied in Tamil up to Class VI.

The couple survived on the paltry sum that Shamsuddin earned and lived in an illegal hut in Bandra where someone else from their village had already settled. There was no electricity, no water. Later, they moved to Kalyanwadi, in Dharavi, where Shamsuddin's uncle had lived. Theirs was the only Muslim house in the middle of about thirty Thevar families from Tamil Nadu. 'But there were no problems,' recalls Shamsuddin.

In 1961, Shamsuddin moved to Kuttiwadi, which was a 'settled chawl'. He paid Rs 475 for a 10 feet by 18 feet room. In those days, he says, there was plenty of water. The municipality would keep the place clean; there was even a separate tap for the cattle. The chawl was named after Hasan Kutti from Kerala who built Badi Masjid in 1887.

'One man from Tirunelvelli, Hamid, knew how to make chiki,' recounts Shamsuddin. 'He came to me and said, "Give me space and I'll make chiki." So we got him a *jhopda* and he began to make mysore pak and chiki. I would take it to the shops and sell it. I left my job at the press as this way I earned much more—a profit of Rs 25 per day.'

In time, Shamsuddin and his wife also learned how to make chiki. As a result, when Hamid left for Calcutta, they took over the business. They would make chiki all day, pack it up in old newspapers, and Shamsuddin would take it to the canteens of cinema halls to sell in the evening. He would return around 11 p.m.

He named his brand A-1 chiki after a chewing gum by the same name manufactured in Calcutta. Shamsuddin's business flourished until the riots of 1992-93, when all his workers ran away. 'That's when I lost interest and handed the business over to one of the boys who used to work for me. He now runs it and gives me a share of the profits each month,' says Shamsuddin.

The A-1 chiki factory is still located in Abu Bakr chawl, Kuttiwadi, off Dharavi Cross Road. Today, it comprises two pucca rooms with lofts. Around twenty workers work in the two gloomy rooms. All of them are from Tirunelvelli district and most of them speak only Tamil. They sleep in the loft above the place where they work. In one room, workers are busy making mysore pak, while in the other masala dal is being fried. The fuel for the stoves is sawdust brought from the timber market in Reay Road. Both rooms have become black with the smoke which billows from the sawdust-fired stoves.

Shamsuddin now lives in Nagri Apartments, one of Dharavi's high-rise buildings. His tiled, plush drawing room has two phones, a wooden cabinet with a TV set, curios kept in a glass cabinet and many other accoutrements of middle-class living. This distinguished looking seventy-year-old, in his white shirt, lungi and white lace cap, speaks Hindi with a pronounced Tamil accent. He has been on Haj and is now known as Haji saheb—Haji P.S. Shamsuddin. His sons are educated and have their own businesses. One of them runs a medical store on Dharavi Main Road.

Haji Shamsuddin's story is not atypical. In fact, Dharavi is full of such stories—of men who went literally from rags to riches in one lifetime. What made it possible? Their own enterprise and hard work? A little bit of luck? Or the compulsions of survival, and the lack of a safety net, that forces people to attempt to do the impossible?

Enterprise and ingenuity

Haji Shamsuddin's story is repeated many times in the lives of the people living in Dharavi. It is a story of ingenuity and enterprise; it is a story of survival without subsidies or welfare; it is a story that illustrates how limited is the term 'slum' to describe a place that produces everything from suitcases to leather goods, Indian sweets, papads and gold jewellery.

Every square inch of Dharavi is being used for some productive activity. This is 'enterprise' personified, an island of free enterprise not assisted or restricted by the State, or any law. It brandishes its illegality. Child labour, hazardous industries, adulteration, recycling, popular products from cold drinks to toothpaste produced in Dharavi—it is all there for anyone to see. Nothing is hidden because people here know that nothing will be done to stop them. Dharavi is an unofficially endorsed enclave of crass illegality that continues to flourish under the tightly shut eyes of the law.

The atmosphere in Dharavi, even on a holiday, is like being on a treadmill. Everyone is busy, doing something. There are few people hanging about. The streets are lined with hawkers selling everything, from safety pins to fruits, and even suitcases. Behind them are a mad array of shops. Satkar jewellers, ration shop, Bhupendra Steel, Husain Hotel, Swastik Electric and Hardware, Shreenath Jewellers and Mumbai Polyclinic— that is a typical collection on 90 Feet Road. Hindu, Muslim, south, north, food, jewellery, hardware, health care, all down one street.

If you want to eat the best gulab jamuns in town, buy the best chiki, acquire an export quality leather handbag, order World Health Organization (WHO) certified sutures for surgery, see the latest design in ready-made garments being manufactured for export, get a new suitcase or an old one repaired, taste food from the north and the south, see traditional south Indian gold jewellery—there are few better places in all of Mumbai than Dharavi. Some of these goods are easy to locate as they are sold in shops on the main streets that criss-cross Dharavi. But much more can be found tucked away in some inner lane that can only be located if you are guided by a Dharavi resident.

Estimates of the daily turnover of Dharavi can only be wild guesses as few people will actually acknowledge how much they earn for fear that some official will descend on them. Much of the production here is illegal. But there is little doubt that it runs into crores of rupees. A rough back-of-the-envelope calculation by Dharavi residents added up to between Rs 1,500 crore and Rs 2,000 crore per year or at least Rs 5 crore a day! And roughly around Rs 11 crore per hectare per year! No wonder people think of Dharavi as a 'gold mine' without even considering property prices.

A 1986 survey of Dharavi by the National Slum Dwellers' Federation (NSDF) confirmed what one can see as one wanders through Dharavi's lanes. At that time, there were 1,044 manufacturing units of all kinds, big and small. A later survey by the Society for Human and Environmental Development (SHED) noted 1,700 units. The actual number is likely to be larger as many smaller units, which work out of homes and lofts, would have fallen outside the scope of the surveys.

The NSDF survey estimated that there were 244 small-scale manufacturers employing from five to ten persons. The forty-three big industries recorded in the survey are probably only medium-scale production units. These would include two factories making sutures—one of them a multinational company—one making what is called 'duplicate colgate', a toothpaste which sports an international brand name ('duplicate' everything is a speciality of Dharavi), soapmaking units, a mithai factory and some of the tanneries that did not shift even though on paper all tanneries were supposed to have been moved out of Dharavi to Deonar by the end of the 1980s.

The NSDF survey recorded 152 units making a variety of food items like chiki, papad, channa dal; fifty printing presses; 111 restaurants; 722 scrap and recycling units; eighty-five units working entirely for export; and twenty-five bakeries. These units are spread out all over Dharavi with big concentrations in Transit Camp.

The common point about all these enterprises, including some of the bigger ones, is that they have come up despite the government, and not because of it.

Few of them receive the benefits that the government offers small- and medium-scale industries. The majority do not abide by laws that apply to these industries. It is a mutually beneficial situation: the government does not have the headache of having to supervise and tax such a diverse 'industrial' sector, and the enterprises can flourish by flouting every law, including that of safe working conditions. Workers have no health insurance, there are constant lay-offs and redundancies as cheaper labour replaces the old, but neither the government, nor the entrepreneurs, nor even the workers, complain because in their own way, everyone gains something from this situation.

It is virtually impossible to capture the diversity of manufacturing activities in Dharavi. But they can roughly be divided into the traditional trades and the more modern ones. The latter include the leather industry—tanneries, finished goods and other leather-related products like sutures, or buckles. Also in this category is the garments industry, most of which sells its products in the local market. Then you have food—sweets, papads and baked products. Dharavi has some of the most hazardous industries, like waste recycling and foundries making brass buckles. In the traditional industries are potters, jewellery makers and gold refiners.

The leather business

Officially, all the tanneries of Dharavi have been relocated to Deonar. In the past, when tanneries dotted Dharavi's landscape, the first thing that hit you was the stench. Ask anyone what they thought of Dharavi during the

Ayesha Taleyarkhan

Precious burden: The leather industry provides jobs to many.

1950s and 1960s and they will tell you that it stank. There were parts of the settlement that were covered with wool fluff from the hides after they were cleaned. Even today, there are lanes in Dharavi that are carpeted with wool from the sheep and goat skins drying in the sun. A small breeze can blow the lighter fluff onto the low rooftops and beyond.

Although twenty-seven out of the thirty-nine tanneries that operated in Dharavi were given alternative land in Deonar, only the larger ones shifted. Some of the small, older tanneries continue to operate in the inner depths of the settlement despite the official ban. Walk through the Tamil-dominated area of Palwadi, for instance, and you will chance upon some sheds. At one end, a former employee of a multinational company has set up a soap factory, producing detergent bars that are strikingly similar to the brand produced by his former employers. And at the other end you see the way leather was treated in the past in Dharavi. The overwhelming presence in the shed is that of an enormous wooden drum that creaks somnolently, like a behemoth which does not know how to stop. Inside its cavernous depths are scores of hides being swilled around in a chemical solution that is almost the last stage in leather processing.

In the old days, those who worked in the tanneries also lived there. The work was incredibly dirty and only men of the lowest castes were employed for the job. The raw hides would arrive from the abattoir at night. They first had to be washed as they would be full of blood. The next stage was to apply salt (sodium sulphide) and leave them for four hours. Then they would be salted one more time. Most of the hides would be sent off at this stage to other tanners.

But in some places, the hides were treated further. They were soaked in lime pits or in drums for four days. This would condition the leather to absorb the chemicals that would be applied later. After this, the hides were shaved—manually at that time, now by machine—to remove the wool and remaining flesh and fat.

The next step was to soak the hides in ammonium chloride, the deliming process. This fixes the leather and also removes any last remnants of hair. The hide becomes almost white at this stage.

Next came the chemical stage where the leather is processed over eight hours in chromium sulphate. It is left aside for one day before fat liquor is applied to the hide to soften it. Only after this process is it dried. The last stage is the dyeing and colouring.

Now that most of the tanneries have moved out of Dharavi; only the first stages of treatment are done there. The semi-processed hides are shipped off to Chennai for the final treatment. The processed hides then return to Dharavi to be crafted into finished products.

The first stage of the leather process is probably the worst. You walk into Kuttiwadi, off Dharavi Main Road, and pass Innayatbhai's godown where the hides are being treated with sodium sulphide. The smell is enough to make you gag. Perhaps, over time you get immune to it. Innayatbhai clearly is not bothered as he sits supervising the work of his men as they apply salt to the hides.

According to Eklakh, 40,000 goats are killed each week in Deonar (on Tuesdays and Saturdays). These animals are brought to Mumbai from Gujarat and Madhya Pradesh. These are the government's official figures of the number of animals slaughtered. But another 5,000 or so are slaughtered 'unofficially'. All these hides are brought to Dharavi for the first stage of processing. Each skin is bought for Rs 100 and resold, after salting, for a slightly higher sum. The margins are very small, says Eklakh. Apart from goats, the abattoir also slaughters 500 buffaloes and 200 cows a week. These skins sell at Rs 500 each.

Most of those dealing in leather are either UP Muslims, or Muslims and Hindus from Tirunelvelli district. The odd man out is Darab Pedar, a genial, bespectacled sixty-seven-year-old Parsi who is more comfortable in Hindi than in English. 'My father brought me into this way of life,' he says. 'We have to sail in the same boats as our fathers. What to do?' he asks rhetorically, a twinkle in his eyes.

The Pedar family's connection with leather goes back to the years before World War I when Darab Pedar's grandfather went to Aden to work in a German company. They would buy skins from Africa, put them through the first stage of processing, and then send them to Germany for the tanning and finishing.

In 1930, Pedar's father came back to India and found a job with a tanner in Dharavi. He worked there till 1957 when he retired, and a year later he died. After retiring, he had started his own business. His untimely death forced Darab Pedar to leave college and take on the business. Until 1978, Pedar worked with the largest leather manufacturer in India, Nagappa Chettiar. Altogether the Chettiar tanneries treat 50,000 skins a day which are supplied from 200 buying centres all over India. Pedar used to manage the fourteen buying centres in the western region.

In 1978, Darab Pedar left Chettiar and started his own business, the Veera Tanneries. As there was no space in Dharavi or Mumbai to establish a tannery, Pedar decided to set it up in Aurangabad, where he acquired sixty-five acres of land in an industrial estate.

Pedar's Dharavi unit procures hides from the Deonar abattoir, puts them through the salting process and sends them to Aurangabad for the rest. He deals in 1,000 to 1,200 hides a day.

Pedar estimates that the annual turnover in the raw leather business in Dharavi is around Rs 60 crore, over Rs 50 crore in sheep and goat hides and the rest in buffalo and cow hides.

While the days of leather tanning are more or less over in Dharavi, finished leather goods have taken over as the main leather-based business. As you come to the end of 90 Feet Road and turn onto the Sion-Mahim link road, you see gleaming leather showrooms with names like Jazz, Leathercraft, Step-in and Ideal Leather on either side of the road. Behind their plate glass windows are displayed the latest designs in leather handbags as well as briefcases and suitcases. Within their air-conditioned confines you find wallets, belts, photo-frames and all manner of leather goods. Many of these are either surplus or rejects from export orders placed with leather goods manufacturers in Dharavi. They sell these goods at half of what you would pay in similar shops in south Mumbai. Bargaining is the norm. Everyone works on narrow margins and is willing to sell the same product for a marginally lower price.

This is the famous leather street that has made Dharavi a name even the rich of Mumbai now know. But the leather processed in Dharavi is usually not of a high enough quality to be used in finished goods. For them, processed leather is trucked in from Chennai, which now has most of the tanneries.

While the finished goods sit in air-conditioned splendour, the men who labour over these products have none of these comforts. They sit instead in cramped lofts or workrooms and work in bad light, poor ventilation and in stifling heat to produce the most beautifully finished and crafted leather goods.

Siddhant Leather Works is one of the oldest finished goods workshops in Dharavi. It is located inconspicuously in a lane behind these flashy showrooms. In a narrow room sits young Manish Mane who runs it now. He inherited it from his grandfather, Shankar Mane, who came to Bombay looking for work in 1933 from the border area of Solapur and Satara districts of Maharashtra. Shankar had worked with leather in his village, as had his father. Thus, he easily found work in the only leather manufacturing unit at that time, the Universal Trading Company, located at Princess Street, where he made leather bags and earned Rs 20 per month.

In 1942, when Hindu-Muslim riots broke out in Bombay, Shankar Mane went back to his village. He only returned in 1946 after peace between the communities had been restored. Fortunately for him, the owner of Universal Trading Company decided to help him set up his own workshop. Thus, in 1951, Mane bought a 36 feet by 12 feet room in Dharavi's Parsi Chawl for Rs 1,800 and established Siddhant Leather Works. Manish and his fifty-five-year-old father, Shivram Shankar Mane, continue to conduct business in this room.

But much has changed in the surroundings. This area was called Parsi Chawl because it was owned by a Parsi. Originally, it consisted of stables for cows, buffaloes and horses. Once the British left, the stables were converted into chawls—single-room tenements with

a loft and a tiled roof. Many of those original structures
have survived. Shivram strengthened and improved his
tenement in 1955 and still has with him the municipal
clearance and approved plans. These contain some quaint
suggestions; for instance, the municipality laid down
that all the windows should be made of teak!

Shivram's former boss gave him one leather sewing
machine with which to start work. In time, he was able
to purchase eight more machines. In those days a
sewing machine would cost between Rs 150 and Rs
200. Today, you have to pay as much as Rs 36,000 for
a machine, and this can go up to Rs 80,000.

Unlike his father, who left school and came to work
in Mumbai, Shivram studied up to Standard XI. He has
two sons and two daughters and has made sure all of
them are educated.

When Shivram began to work out of Dharavi, there
were only two others doing the same work. Today,
there are between twenty-five and thirty larger leather
goods manufacturers in Dharavi while there are more
than 5,000 doing jobwork. These are people with one
or two machines who work out of their homes on the
basis of orders they get from bigger businesses. Shivram
estimates that in the area where they live, almost every
home has one or two people doing jobwork.

The workshop has six men making jewellery boxes
on the ground floor and three boys in the loft making
parts for leather briefcases. Aftab is a seventeen-year-
old from Madhubani district in Bihar who is busily
making the parts. He says, 'When I first came to
Mumbai, I lived with a relative. I somehow managed to
find work and realized how nice it was to have money.

As a result, I decided it wasn't worth going back to my studies in Bihar.' Altaf is typical of the bright and precocious boys you meet in such workshops in Dharavi. He has an opinion on everything: 'Laloo cares for the poor, that is why he is popular,' he says about Bihar's colourful former chief minister.

Shivram points out that the place where the shops stand today was marshland when he came to live in Parsi Chawl with his father. At that time, the majority of those working in finished leather goods, which included many making chappals and shoes, were Maharashtrians. A substantial number were from the Satara area. Today, Shivram says 60 per cent of those doing this work are Muslims, from UP and Bihar. The Maharashtrians like Shivram who are still in the leather business make mostly bags and wallets. Very few use their traditional skill of making chappals and shoes. You have to search the lanes to find such a person.

One such person is Damodar Ramachandra Kamble, who runs a shoe workshop in Parsi Chawl. He established the Jaishree Leather Art in 1982 and concentrates on export orders that require him to make just 'uppers'. These are then sent to a factory where the sole is added. The shoes are then exported to Australia and Japan.

Kamble claims he is the only person in Dharavi doing this type of work. He has about twenty workers spread over a room of around 10 feet by 20 feet and a loft—quite spacious by Dharavi standards. The work area is also well-lit and not stuffy like the other workshops. His workers come from all parts of India, including UP and Bihar.

Kamble, who is from Neena village in Pune district,

says his parents also worked on footwear. 'Our circumstances were bad, so we had to come to Mumbai. I used to be a worker for fifteen years in a leather factory. I started this business with no workers. Then gradually I employed more people. Today, I have an annual turnover of Rs 1 crore,' he says proudly.

Proximity to the abattoir in Bandra also produced another trade—that of making sutures. Apart from Johnson and Johnson, the multinational company which has a factory in Dharavi, the other person best known in this trade is Abdul Baqua who runs the Ideal Trading Company. His factory has been certified by WHO and he is proud that despite the filth of Dharavi, his factory can maintain the highest standards of hygiene and manufacture sutures that are meant exclusively for export.

Baqua's story is one of the many success stories that one constantly encounters in Dharavi. He came from Azamgarh district in 1948 at the age of thirteen. He knew no one in Dharavi but had to leave his village because his father had died when he was just two years old. Although his mother married again, they were financially in dire straits.

'I heard there were some people from Azamgarh in Dharavi. So I came here and slept in the mosque, in Badi Masjid. During the day I worked as a cleaning boy at Rafiq UP Restaurant across the road for Rs 15 a month. I worked there for four years, until 1952, and saved absolutely nothing. Dharavi was terrible in those days. It was a swamp. We had to wade through it to come from Mahim station,' recalls Baqua.

Discouraged by this, Baqua went back to Azamgarh

in 1952 where he set up a ration shop. Ten years of selling provisions got him nowhere. In 1962, Baqua came back to Bombay to try his luck again but did not bring his family. He had no funds to start a business. A friend who had gone to Coimbatore, where he was manufacturing sutures, asked Baqua to join him there. In time, Baqua mastered the trade. He was able to launch out on his own and began making sutures which were sold to big companies like Johnson and Johnson and also exported. Within three years, Baqua had managed to accumulate enough capital to buy a proper house and live comfortably in Coimbatore.

One of the companies to which he supplied sutures was an Italian company based in Bombay. The owner, an Italian Jew, invited Baqua to work with him in Bombay. They went into partnership and worked for some years exporting sutures. In 1970, the Italian said he wanted to move back to Italy and had no interest in continuing the business. Baqua took over his orders and set up a factory in Dharavi in 1970 registered as the Ideal Trading Company.

Thus, Baqua's sutures complete the circle of the leather business—from hides, to finished goods, to sutures. Each of these has a place in Dharavi because of the original location of the abattoir at Bandra. Despite the other changes that have taken place in the city, and in Dharavi, the leather business continues to be the dominant trade with which Dharavi is associated.

Shirt off your back

Off Dharavi Cross Road, a slushy lane opens out into Kuttiwadi. On one side are the oldest bakeries of

Dharavi. On the other are a row of godowns. The first
is one of the primitive leather processing units that can
be found in many lanes of Dharavi, identifiable by the
stench that escapes through their open doors.

The next godown, by contrast, is a garments factory.
There are three long tables ready for the master cutters,
the paper patterns pinned to the walls, the bales of cloth
on one side. Mustaqeem, a bespectacled young man in
kurta-pyjama and white sandals, sits in a small air-
conditioned cabin at one end. The cabin next to him has
a computer which connects him to markets in distant
US. On his desk are phones, a fax, and on the side is a
rack with samples of ready-made garments. Mustaqeem
exports garments to the US where they are ultimately
sold through Wal-Mart and Kmart.

But in 1970, when Mustaqeem came to Bombay as
a lad of thirteen from UP, he did not dream that one
day he would own a garments factory and export
directly to the US. His family members were landowners
in UP's Rae Bareli district, better known as the
constituency of the Nehru-Gandhi dynasty. Over time,
with the division of land, the family was reduced to
penury. This forced Mustaqeem to venture out, looking
for work in Bombay, even though he had not completed
his school education.

His first home in the big city was in the disreputable
Kamathipura area, better known as Bombay's red-light
district. A relative who lived there allowed him to stay
with him. Mustaqeem started work in a ready-made
garments factory where he was not paid but given the
chance to learn the trade. Every morning he would go
there at 7.30, clean the place, wash the machines, serve

tea to the workers and then hang around till everyone left. Only after that could he try the machines and learn how to sew. All the workers were from UP and as they had no place to live, they usually slept on the road outside the factory. Within four months, he had learned how to stitch on the pedal machines and become a good tailor. 'My motto was that if I work hard, God will honour me. I would tell the workers that one day I too would own a factory.'

In 1974, Mustaqeem managed to persuade a relative who lived in Dharavi to let him put two sewing machines in his home. Mustaqeem operated one machine and hired a man to run the other. They worked all day and would somehow manage to find jobwork. But expenses were often higher than what they earned. So, while in the past he could send some money home as he earned a regular salary in a garments factory, he could not do this once he began his own business.

But slowly, he says, he was able to expand and eventually had ten machines placed in additional rooms that he managed to rent. The men who worked there stayed in these rooms. At this stage he felt confident to ask two of his brothers to come to the city to help him while the third stayed behind to look after the land. Today, Mustaqeem exudes prosperity even though he still operates out of a shed in Kuttiwadi which becomes unapproachable after a downpour.

There are only a couple of other garments exporters in Dharavi but there are dozens who take on jobwork for exporters. They are around every corner in the rebuilt Chamda Bazaar or Bageecha area which was razed to the ground during the 1992-93 riots. But the majority of garment manufacturers in Dharavi cater to the local market.

They include men like Haji Abdul Haq Ansari, who was forced to move his workshop to Dharavi when his factory in Mazgaon was burnt during the riots. During that time he was imprisoned and his hands broken. The bitterness has not gone and the sadness is evident in his eyes, in his body language.

Today, Ansari has a workshop in Indira Kureishi Nagar, another of the many nagars off Dharavi's 90 Feet Road. Once you enter it through a narrow lane, you find yourself transported to another part of India. This is not just a part of Uttar Pradesh but a specific district in that state, Gonda. Like Ansari, the majority of people living and working in Indira Kureishi Nagar are from there.

Among them is twelve-year-old Jameel, who sits cleaning an embroidered material. He works for twelve hours, sleeps and eats in the workshop, has no problems about having left his native place to live in this squalor. What will he do when he grows up? 'Maybe I'll also own a factory,' he says, not an unrealistic dream given the number of people you meet who have done precisely this.

Jameel's boss, Ansari, came to Mumbai from UP in 1965 and began doing small stitching jobs. Now he has several machines and workers and gets job orders from exporters. He says he is one of the smaller jobbers and can make around Rs 7 lakh per year. The bigger ones, he feels, can make double that amount. In his Shalimar society of seventy people, formed post-riots with people from Gonda ('So that we can protect each other against harassment and extortion'), half the members are big jobbers. Ansari turns out 500 to 600 shirts a day. Workers are paid on a piece-rate basis and can earn up to Rs 150 per day. They are mostly from Bihar and some from Tamil Nadu. Ansari thinks there must be at least 500 people like him doing jobwork in Dharavi and another 100 doing hand embroidery called zardozi and machine embroidery.

The zardozi work requires great skill and is usually done by young boys from Bengal and Bihar. You find them sitting on the floor with a piece of cloth tautly stretched before them on a rack, doing intricate embroidery with gold and silver threads. It is painstaking work, often done in bad light. As with other trades, the workmen eat, sleep and work in the same space.

You also come across men busy doing machine embroidery. It appears that the majority of men in this trade are from Bengal. The constant and virtually non-stop whirring of machines can usually lead you to one of these workshops. The machine embroidery is mostly done for the local market.

Dharavi's garments business, unlike the leather trade, seems to have remained immune to the ups and downs of the export trade because it caters mainly to the local market. You will find evidence of this in one of the lanes of Social Nagar where there are over a dozen shops on either side selling cloth and ready-mades. This is your typical souk, your *kapda* bazaar that can be found anywhere in India. Daylight never reaches the lane separating the shops. All the shops have tubelights, fans, linoleum floors and some, like Waqar Khan Pyare's, have fancy shelves packed with shirts.

Here's another of Dharavi's rags-to-riches stories. Waqar, who had studied up to Standard VIII in his village in Bareilly district in UP, came to Bombay in 1978 when he was thirteen years old. His family once had a lot of landed property. But they had gradually sold their land to survive. Left with too little for all of them—his parents, two brothers and two sisters—to live on, Waqar, the eldest, was sent to Bombay where he lived with an uncle in Dharavi.

Waqar began working by buying and selling bananas. He did this for a year. Then he found a job selling ready-made garments in front of Dadar Station. Like other unauthorized hawkers, Waqar had to contend with daily harassment from municipal workers. But he somehow stuck on with the job and put some money aside.

With this money he rented two sewing machines. He set these up in the room where he lived, rented for Rs 5 per month, and started taking on jobwork. He was lucky to find a client who gave him regular work. He realized that there was a lucrative local market which could be supplied. Today, with twelve workers and three shops, Waqar sells shirts all over India and has a turnover of Rs 70 lakh a year.

Food, glorious food

You can hide garment units in lofts but you cannot hide the smell of food. Imagine the overpowering smell of ghee assaulting you as you make your way through one of the many garbage-encrusted roads in Dharavi. If you look behind the high gates next to Diamond Apartments, where Abdul Baqua, who makes sutures, lives, you will see a factory-like structure set within a large compound.

This is the place where gulab jamuns, rosogullas, chamchams, motichoor ladoos, kaju barfee and many more delectable Indian sweets are made. The next time you bite into a soft, sweet, gulab jamun at a five-star hotel in Mumbai, you will probably be eating something manufactured in Dharavi.

Punjabi Ghasitaram Halwai Karachiwala is located today in what was the Diamond Aerating Works, a soda water factory that was built in 1949. Ghasitaram moved to this spot in 1978 from another location in Bombay. The business was founded by Govardhandas Ghasitaram Bajaj who had come from Karachi after Partition. He had decided to continue with the sweet business in independent India. His family had run a similar business in Karachi since 1916. His sons continued the business but split in 1978. One of the brothers now has the factory in Dharavi.

Mohan Katre, the manager of the factory, takes great pride in every aspect of his work and has been with the Bajaj family since 1951, when they began with a small sweetshop in Kalbadevi. Theirs is the biggest Indian sweets manufacturing factory in Mumbai and possibly in India, says Katre.

The factory remains as it was when the Diamond Aerating Works owned it. In a huge cavernous high-ceilinged hall, there are groups of workers doing different things. At one end are six stainless steel boilers for heating the milk. On the side are iron kadais, where the milk is converted into khoya for Bengali sweets and for gulab jamuns. The factory uses 2,000 litres of buffalo milk and 800 litres of cow milk every day which arrives at the factory gates from Vasai, Dahisar and Turbhe, on the outskirts of Mumbai.

The most interesting aspect of the trade is that each set of workers comes from a different part of India. Thus, Bengali workers make chamchams and rosogullas, Punjabis make ladoos and gulab jamuns, Maharashtrians make kaju katris and barfees and the UP bhaiyas make khoya and milk-based sweets as well as some of the savouries, like samosas. Katre says it is best to use people from the region where the sweets originate as they know how to make them.

Ghasitaram employs around 200 workers who live in the compound or just across it. During the 1992-93 riots, the factory was not affected because the workers were right there. The owners had the foresight to keep the police happy. They fed 200 policemen every day at the height of the riots. As a result, they got police escort for their vans when the sweets were ready for delivery.

A bigger food business is that of manufacturing chiki, channa, chakli and mysore pak. If you walk down Dharavi Cross Road, you will find on either side shops laden with goods which have been manufactured and packed in the homes and lanes just behind these shops.

Until 1992-93, Hindu and Muslim Tamils identified themselves with their region and not their religion. The riots changed all that. Even if Tamil did not turn on Tamil, the fact that Hindu Tamilians attacked UP Muslims or vice versa polarized the Tamil community along religious lines.

The exceptions are the chiki-makers of Dharavi. Of

the twenty-seven involved in making chiki, only one, Haji Shamsuddin, is a Muslim. But he is the oldest and is respected as a father of the tribe. The others turn to him for advice and for help to settle even domestic disputes.

Dharavi's chiki-makers produce tons of the peanut brittle which is sold all over the city and outside. Ramaswamy from Tirunelvelli district, for instance, lives in Kamaraj Nagar, which is an enclave of people from his district. His daughter, Selvy, is now studying to become a chartered accountant. Yet his wife speaks hardly any other language except Tamil and is afraid to speak to strangers. In one generation, there has been such a remarkable change—all from the profits of chiki.

In addition to chiki and mithai, you will see many women rolling out papads. Some of them are supplying them to Lijjat papad. This is a women's organization called Shri Mahila Griha Udyog Lijjat Papad. It began in 1959 with a few women in central Bombay rolling out papads to earn some extra money. It has now grown to an organization with 40,000 members throughout India. Lijjat has 8,000 registered members in Mumbai, of whom around fifty live in Dharavi. These women travel to Bandra every day to collect the wet dough from which papads are made. Within a couple of days, they are back with the rolled out papads which have been dried in the sun. For their efforts, these women earn an average of Rs 50 to Rs 60 per day.

Of course, not all the women you see rolling out papads are part of Lijjat. Many do this for private entrepreneurs and are probably not paid as much. There is also little supervision of their work. As a result, you often see the papads, which are dried in the sun on upturned baskets, sitting next to a garbage dump, or covered with flies. The Lijjat organizers insist that their members have to take care to maintain hygiene and that there are frequent inspections.

Brun, butter and pav

Modern methods have not touched the manufacture of most of the food produced in Dharavi. Thus, despite the availability of electricity and gas, all the bakeries in Dharavi continue to use wood-fired ovens, something they have done for more than fifty years.

Eighty-year-old Haji Abdul Shakur Jamaluddin is one of the oldest bakers of Dharavi. He owns the Maqdoomia Bakery which was started in 1952 just after the Nagina Bakery. Even at this age, he visits the bakery twice a day.

If Jamaluddin's story sounds familiar by now, it is. Like so many others, Jamaluddin's father came to Bombay in 1928 from Mohammadabad in UP's Bijnore district. He found a job in a bakery and learned the trade. Ten years later, Jamaluddin came to Bombay and went to school in the city. In 1952, his father bought a godown in Dharavi's Abu Bakr Chawl and set up the Maqdoomia Bakery. It has two ovens and bakes bread, butter (a savoury biscuit popularized by the Irani bakers), toast (sweet rusk) and bun. Every day, it bakes around 270 kg of these items.

Behind Maqdoomia, on Dharavi Main Road, is Mamu's Bakery. Forty-five-year-old Abdul Aziz Khan, better known as Mamu, 'owns' a large compound just off Dharavi Main Road. If you ask him whether he actually owns it, he quickly 'disowns' it. He's only a tenant, he says, and has a Muslim landlady. But for all purposes he owns this strategically located plot which has residential quarters on two sides and a bakery on the other two.

Mamu's Bakery is well known in Dharavi. The compound where his bakery is presently located was earlier a tannery. Unlike Jamaluddin, Mamu is not a baker by profession. He made his money in the firewood trade at the height of the illicit liquor era. Dharavi was the main brewing ground for country liquor, and firewood was needed for the stills. Apart from the liquor stills, hundreds of tons of firewood was needed for the bakeries.

Rafeeq Ellias

Mamu's Bakery: With the help of two large wood-fired ovens, Mamu's workers turn out golden brown pav and other delicacies.

Mamu estimates that there were between fifteen and sixteen large liquor stills in those days and at least fifty smaller ones. The bigger ones would produce at least 100 tubes of liquor a day and one tube could carry around fifteen litres. A rough calculation suggests that if all the stills were working to full capacity, Dharavi would have produced around 25,000 litres of its deadly illicit brew each day.

When the police finally decided to crack down on the liquor business in Dharavi, Mamu switched professions and became a baker. Today, he has two large wood-fired ovens in his bakery and bakes brun (a hard-crusted bun) and slice bread (a regular loaf) in the night. These are supplied early in the morning to restaurants where people have Mumbai's special bun-maska (bun with butter) and chai before going to work. Mamu's Bakery also produces 150 kg of khari and 100 kg of butter biscuits during the day.

Mamu's workers are mostly from Azamgarh district. All of them are on daily wages, there are no permanent employees. The best paid are those who tend the ovens. They earn as much as Rs 80 per day and are in great demand. As a result, they rarely stick to one job. The next most skilled are those who knead and make the dough. The rest, the packers and cleaners, which include women, get paid only around Rs 25 per day.

The scene inside Mamu's Bakery is almost surreal. You see men dressed in loose cotton pyjamas and vests stoking the ovens and kneading the dough on long stone slabs. At the other end of the room, men and some women are greasing the trays in which the moulds of dough will be placed. Everyone works in unison; not a word is spoken. Each knows his or her task. So as the men cut and mould the dough, another team places each item carefully in the greased trays. Two men put the trays at the edge of the two ovens and push them in with long iron rods. By instinct, they seem to know when to pull the trays out. The trays of perfect, golden brown pav, or khari, or butter, are then left to cool before being packed in polythene.

The baked goods are sent either through *pheriwalas*, who go on foot with a tin box on their heads carrying freshly baked biscuits, or the cyclewallahs, who balance a tray at the back and two large bags packed with bread on either side of the handlebar. Most of these men are from UP although some are from the south. The new recruits are all Biharis. Each bakery has a group of *pheriwalas* attached to it. They get a place to sleep and, in return, they buy and sell the products.

In 1952, when Jamaluddin began his bakery, there were two other bakers. Today, there are over twenty-five in Dharavi. Most of them have two wood-fired ovens. At dawn, a pall of smoke hovers over the area where these bakeries are located. Residents complain but nothing is done. Controlling pollution is not a major preoccupation for people living in Dharavi.

Smoke and fire

In Mukand Nagar, the smoke and fire is inside the rooms. If there is hell, you will find it in a narrow lane in this part of Dharavi where primitive foundries fashion brass buckles for leather belts and bags.

No one here has ever heard about labour standards or occupational health hazards. Such concepts have never interfered with a day's work in these production units that hark back to the beginning of the industrial era. All you need is a room, a hole, some coal, some sand and motor oil and poor men willing to destroy their lungs.

The lane we walk down is barely three feet wide. On either side are dark, soot-covered rooms, 8 feet by 6 feet, the hell-holes that are integral to the buckle trade. As you enter the room, you see a square pit with glowing embers. It is covered with an iron grill on which are placed burning coals. The fire blazes. An earthenware pot with pieces of brass is placed on the hot coals. The heat eventually melts the metal. The smoke from the pit fills the room. Through the haze you can see four figures, young men who are working using a medieval method to forge buckles out of this molten brass. Most of them are from UP. All of them say they will do this until they find some other work. None of them see this as their life's vocation.

Scores of moulds, boxes filled with a mixture of sand and motor oil, are scattered around the room. Each box has an impress on either side made with a mould. Several such moulds hang on the wall. When the brass melts, it is poured by one man into the mould. He closes the box, waits for a few seconds, opens it, and pries out the strip of brass buckles with a pair of thongs. The second boy picks up the strip with thongs, and pries each buckle loose and throws them into a tray. They are still too hot to touch. The middle strip which holds the twelve buckles together is thrown back on the fire to melt.

The tray full of buckles is then taken across the lane

to the buffing unit where three men carefully polish each buckle till it gleams like gold. A day's work from one *bhatti* (foundry) can produce 1,200 or more buckles. The finished products are placed in plastic bags and taken to the *dhani* (owner) who waits at the end of this lane.

The *dhani* is Iliyasbhai, an ansari (weaver) from Moradabad in UP who has now become a brass worker. Moradabad is famous for brass but Iliyasbhai's family was not involved in it. Tall, dark and swarthy, he is often mistaken for a 'Madrasi'. In fact, this is why he is called Anna in the neighbourhood.

This dark and dingy lane in Mukand Nagar is home to several workshops making buckles and buffing units. The only people living there are those who work in these units. The dour expression on their faces tells you the real story of their lives. If you show an interest in their lives and in their work, they want to talk. While Iliyasbhai claims that his workers are paid Rs 200 a day, one of the workers says that they make, at the most, Rs 1,200 a month because they only get work for fifteen days in a month.

What happens when they fall ill? The instant reply is: the *dhani* takes care of us. But a moment later, one of them comes up and mumbles, 'Didi, if you want to know the truth, the *dhani* does nothing for us. If we fall ill, we have to fend for ourselves.'

This fear of speaking up about their working conditions also ensures that these workers can never be unionized. If they object to the working conditions, their boss will find ten other workers waiting to take their place. There is no shortage of labour in Mumbai.

So if you have a job, you hold on to it, until you can get a better alternative. Such an attitude is an automatic guarantee against unionization, and against improvement in working conditions.

These workers are breathing in pure poison every day—sulphur dioxide, nitrogen oxide as well as particulate matter which could include, aside from copper and iron oxides, oxides of arsenic, antimony, cadmium, lead, mercury and zinc. Do they realize this? 'We place a piece of jaggery in our mouths and that takes care of the cough,' one young worker tells me philosophically. But what is the colour of their lungs? How long will they live if they continue to work here? No one knows or cares.

The buckle foundries are only one example of the hazardous industries that are hidden within the Dharavi complex. They remain obscured from view; they flourish because no one objects, least of all those who suffer serious health damage from working in them. Some efforts have been made by non-governmental organizations and even trade unions to expose the conditions in these sweatshops. But nothing comes of it because the people on whose behalf the battle is being fought are not interested in being a part of it. They want to live for today so that they can find a better alternative tomorrow.

Recycling everything

Scrapyards are as hellish and degrading as the foundries of Mukand Nagar. But at least you can see the daylight. Recycling waste is a multimillion rupee business in

Mumbai. Dharavi's speciality is recycling plastic. According to the NSDF survey, Dharavi's plastic recycling industry is the largest in India. It employs over 5,000 people and the turnover in 1986 was an estimated Rs 60 lakh a year. Today, it should be many times higher. Every day, at least 3,000 sacks of plastic leave this area.

Ayesha Taleyarkhan

Recycling aluminium: Recycling waste is a lucrative business in Dharavi. Most recycling units are small set-ups.

The recycling and scrap area of Dharavi is concentrated in what is commonly known as 13th Compound, located on the corner where 60 Feet Road meets the Mahim-Sion link road. Across the road is the Mithi river and the Mahim creek, ostensibly an environmentally sensitive area which is supposed to be preserved. In fact, it is a dumping ground. If you go back in the course of a year, you will find a good part of the swamp next to the road has been filled. In another six months, huts will spring up on this reclaimed

land. And so Dharavi will extend a little more to the
north and the new entrants into Dharavi will live in this
swamp, much as their forebears in the rest of the
settlement did five decades back.

But Sanola, Jaleel and Banwari compounds, which
are some of the settlements that comprise 13th
Compound, did not emerge from the marsh yesterday.
They lie east of the railway track that runs past Mahim
to Bandra and were solid ground for several decades.
This is one area that could have been developed, either
as an industrial area, or as a residential one, if the
authorities had been alert. Just when Dharavi's
development began in 1986, a huge fire devastated this
area. It was an opportunity to start from scratch. But
like so many other opportunities, this too was missed.
The area was left alone, and soon the surviving settlement
was overtaken by recycling sheds. Today, both live in
an uneasy alliance. Neither is willing to move or make
a change.

I am taken to Sanola Compound with the promise
that I will see how motor oil is refined so that all the
smells disappear. This oil is then apparently sold for the
singular purpose of adulterating edible oils. But, of
course, if indeed this is done, no one will admit it.
Instead, I am taken on a tour of the recycling business—
oil, plastics, chemical drums, anything.

Nizamuddin from Azamgarh district was one of the
first to set up the oil recycling business in Dharavi. He
came to Mumbai in 1963. He says he only has a small
business. There are fifteen others doing the same business
in 13th Compound.

Nizamuddin buys around forty to fifty drums of oil

(each contains 210 litres) a month from companies and garages. This is discarded motor oil. His job is merely to store these drums and resell them for a small profit to traders who filter it again. The recycled oil is used for such legitimate purposes as in tarmac for roads and several illegitimate purposes which no one is willing to admit.

A few sheds away from Nizamuddin's is a large shed where plastic is being recycled. This is just one of the 121 such sheds in the compound. On one side lie sacks of plastic waste. The recyclers—both men and women—sit in a row on their haunches. Placed in front of them are plastic basins. Without looking up, they sort out the plastic and throw toothbrushes, syringes and other pieces that are whole into separate basins. None of the recyclers wear gloves; none of them know that syringes, in particular, should not be recycled. Blindly, like automatons they separate the waste. The coloured plastic pieces are passed through a machine which breaks them into tiny pieces. This is then sold by weight to plastic manufacturers. The recyclers are paid daily wages of Rs 40 to Rs 45 per day for eleven hours of work.

Just outside the shed, where the plastic is being separated, are stacked large blue drums with the symbol of a well-known multinational company. Companies send their drums for repair and after paying a small amount, get them back ready to be reused. The badly damaged ones are recycled. Next to plastic recycling, the drum recycling business is the biggest—with 145 establishments doing this. But what about the remnants of hazardous chemicals that might still be in these

Ayesha Taleyarkhan

Hazardous work: One of Dharavi's speciality is recycling plastic. Workers separate the plastic waste with their bare hands.

drums? Do the workers handling them protect themselves? Such questions are never asked. Indeed, they never occur to the people running the businesses. And clearly, the multinational companies getting the work done at Sanola Compound could not care less. After all, their hands are clean and they can show that they take good care of all their workers. What is done outside their factory premises, even for jobs done for them, is not their responsibility. So a little bit of First World-Third World politics is on display right here in Sanola Compound, in Dharavi, in Mumbai.

In the 13th Compound, everything is recycled. Cotton scrap, iron scrap, empty tins, empty bottles and plastic

drums. Of the 722 small and big establishments, only
359 are licensed. The majority are small set-ups working
out of lofts. A surprising fact that emerged from the
NSDF survey was the absence of child labour, so
common in the rest of Dharavi and particularly in the
recycling industry in the rest of the city. Here, the
majority of workers were between the ages of twenty-
one and fifty. But as all the workers are on daily wages,
it is possible that some of this information is not
entirely representative as the composition of the
workforce would keep changing.

The land on which these compounds are located
belongs to the municipal corporation. About half the
godown owners have a photopass (or passport as it is
called) and are charged a rent. Nizamuddin hopes that
this means that eventually they will get a better working
area. But no one really knows the future of this business.
Tomorrow, this too might disappear, as did the tanneries,
and make way for more housing because of its prime
location.

The potter's wheel

In contrast to those who manufacture buckles or those
who deal in marketing of scrap, the Kumbhars of
Dharavi have an easier time. At least they have more
space. But their life is hard, and there is no pot of gold
at the end of their rainbow.

Ramjibhai Pithabhai Patel, born in Dharavi's
Kumbharwada, represents six generations from
Saurashtra who have lived and worked in Mumbai.

They came from Junagadh, Verawal and Una.

Kumbharwada occupies twelve and a half acres of prime property in Dharavi. It is strategically located at the point where 90 Feet Road meets 60 Feet Road. Over 250 potters work in this area but there are many more families living there. Apart from the Kumbhars, some houses are also occupied by UP Muslims and some by Maharashtrians who are not in the trade.

Ramjibhai usually has no time to stop and talk to people. Today, he is relaxing. It is Ekadashi, the one day when the Kumbhars do not run their potters' wheels. The room where we meet serves both as a kitchen and a bedroom. A child, Ramjibhai's grandchild, is crying inconsolably in his cradle while his wife, sixty-year-old Motibai, who only speaks the Kathiawadi dialect, makes tea.

Why did his ancestors come to Bombay? 'There was no work there,' explains Ramjibhai. 'The first Kumbharwada was at Naigaun in front of Chitra Cinema (in central Bombay). The government removed them from there to Sion (north of Dharavi). There a military camp came up, so they were then removed to Dharavi in the 1930s. In 1932, all the huts of the Kumbhars got burnt. One Velji Lakhu Seth saw what had happened. We told him that all we wanted was houses, we would manage the rest ourselves.'

So, according to Ramjibhai, Lakhu Seth got contributions from various business houses like the Birlas and the Tatas, and helped the Kumbhars to build their houses in their present location. Ramjibhai was born in the house built then by his father. He now lives there with his wife, their four sons, their wives and ten grandchildren.

'When I was growing up, this was an open space. People used to be afraid to come to Dharavi. They thought of it as a jungle. From here we could see Mahim station. We had a *sangathan* of Kathiawadis, so we felt quite safe. Things began to change around forty years ago when people from outside came.'

Ramjibhai's house is big compared to other houses in Dharavi. 'We need space to keep our mud, make the pots and have a *bhatti*. We have a backyard where several families share a kiln,' explains Ramjibhai.

In 1932, there were 319 Kumbhar families, today there are 2,000. The population of Kumbhars increased after 1947 when many of them left Junagadh and moved to Bombay. The Kumbhars already settled in Bombay accommodated the newcomers.

Life has never been easy for this community. Ramjibhai says that he has to work from seven in the morning to seven at night. In the old days, he would carry the pots he had made to Dadar (not far from Dharavi) to try and sell them. Based on what he sold, he would stop at a grain shop and buy his daily provisions. Thus, they lived on their daily earnings. The whole family was involved in the work.

Today, he says, they are slightly better off, as they can afford to hire workers to light the kilns. Plus, there are merchants who place orders for pots and buy from them directly. So they do not have to worry about selling their products. But because of this, the Kumbhars have not innovated or changed their designs. Barring a couple of enterprising Kumbhars who have learnt new techniques and designs, the majority produce the traditional pots for plants and matkas for keeping water.

Also, although the physical labour of making pots has lessened because of the workers who light the kilns, the Kumbhars now face greater difficulties in obtaining the raw material for making pots. 'In the old days we used to get our mud from Parla and Andheri (suburbs of Mumbai),' says Ramjibhai. 'Now, we have to go to Palghar and Virar and much further. We face lots of difficulties in getting the mud.'

These difficulties, however, dim in comparison to those faced by the few Muslim potters who are also part of Kumbharwada. For generations, Hindu and Muslim potters lived together without conflict. The equations changed all of a sudden in 1992, when events in distant Ayodhya set the city of Mumbai on fire, dividing old neighbours and friends from each other, shattering camaraderie built upon common trades and interests.

One man whose life has changed since the riots lives just a few houses away from Ramjibhai. Ismail Khamisa, aged fifty-five, is one of forty Muslim Kumbhars. All of them come from Kutch and speak Kutchi as opposed to the Hindu Kumbhars who come from north Gujarat and speak Gujarati. Ismailbhai comes from Ratadiya village, but says he hardly knows about Kutch as he was born and brought up in the very house where he now lives and works in Kumbharwada.

Ismailbhai is a disheartened man. He says he hardly mixes with anyone and only does his work. Clearly, the riots changed a great deal in Kumbharwada when the police entered the locality and fired at the closely arranged houses. A visitor from the Konkan, who happened to be staying with Ismailbhai's neighbour, died in the shooting when he stepped out to go to the toilet.

Ismailbhai's grandfather was one of the early potters from Kutch who came to Bombay. They were four or five families who lived in Matunga. The government moved all of them to Kumbharwada and Ismailbhai has lived here ever since.

Ismailbhai has studied up to Class VII. One of his sons has been to college, the other is working with him, and both his daughters are married. He lives in a house next to two of his brothers.

After about four hours of work each morning, Ismailbhai and his son manage to make around 100 large garden pots. These are bought by a trader who gives them a fixed price. Ismailbhai cannot be bothered about marketing. He acknowledges that with more training, they could earn more. The Kumbhars are one of the communities in Dharavi who have remained poor.

Lanes of gold

Sakinabai Chawl is one of Dharavi's oldest chawls, located off Dharavi Main Road, not far from Koliwada. Its narrow lanes are literally lined with gold—refined gold. Here, hidden from the outside world, is the home of gold refining, jewellery making and polishing.

In a small room sit four men, all from Sangli district. At the moment they have no work. At the entrance of the room is a coal-fired stove with a chimney above it, much like the old fireplaces. It also has mechanized bellows on the side. And the chimney, made of aluminium, runs along the side of the room to the top. No smoke enters this room. It comes as a surprise to find an environmentally-friendly workplace in the heart of Dharavi. What a difference from the foundries of Mukand Nagar.

The men explain the process. Gold is kept in small earthenware pots which are then placed in a small opening above the fire. Once the gold melts, it is made into a nugget and weighed. It is sold according to its weight to the jewellers. The gold that is thus smelted is from old ornaments, sold to pay off debts, or to buy new jewellery.

Across the lane sit three young boys, all jewellery makers from Bengal. They are squatting on the ground in front of low wooden tables. Their leader, Dilip, is probably not more than twenty years old. He has a pipe in his mouth through which he blows on hot coals kept in a carved out wooden pot. He is melting down little bits of gold. The molten gold will then be poured into a mould. And before long, Dilip will have produced another piece of gold jewellery. He shows us a pair of intricate gold earrings that he has just completed. Necklaces, pendants and rings are among the ornaments that they make.

Dilip's finished ornaments will be sent for polishing to another part of Sakinabai Chawl to either Todi from Thanjavur or Peer Mohammad from North Arcot. Both men operate out of narrow spaces which open out on the road. They live in lofts above these spaces.

The polishing of gold jewellery is done manually.

One plastic basin has soapy areetha (an astringent berry) water in which the ornament is soaked. The excess dirt is then removed carefully with a brush. Next, without gloves, the men dip the ornament in a solution made of potassium cyanide. When I exclaim about the fact that this is dangerous, both acknowledge the danger but say that they are so used to this that they don't think about it.

Just outside this jewellery-making centre, on the main road, are rows of shops selling jewellery. The designs are deliberately aimed at their primary market, that of Tamilians. And even though most of the shops are owned by Gujaratis, all the signboards are in Tamil. Thus, in one trade you have people from various states—Maharashtra, Gujarat, Bengal and Tamil Nadu—and different religions, Hindu and Muslim. Interestingly, Sakinabai Chawl was one of the areas in Dharavi where the few Muslim families living there were protected by their Hindu neighbours during the riots.

New industries, new recruits

The expected and the unexpected are both manufactured in Dharavi. Thus, bakeries or pots are no surprise. But soap? There are three or four 'factories' manufacturing soap in Dharavi, much of which is sold locally. One such soapmaker is Arumai Nayakam who used to work in the Sewri soap factory of Hindustan Lever Limited (HLL), a job he inherited from his father who retired from the company in 1979. In 1989, when the company declared a lockout, Nayakam thought the time had come for him to move out. He used what he had

Ayesha Taleyarkhan

Making soap: There are three or four units manufacturing soap in Dharavi, much of which is sold locally.

learned as a worker in the HLL factory to set up his own cottage industry.

Today, he produces two tons of detergent cakes per day, and markets them under various names—Radha, Zama and Sofil. The soaps bear an unmistakable resemblance to the brands marketed by HLL and other multinationals but cost less than a quarter of the price. In Dharavi, Nayakam has an assured market for his products.

His factory employs workers on daily wages and piece-rates. The women pack the cakes of soaps which are manufactured in a small room with a couple of machines operated by about a dozen men. Interestingly, the workers of HLL had also resorted to soap manufacture to register their protest against the lockout.

In fact, the soap was called Lockout and was sold to raise funds for the union!

Like Nayakam's soap, you find local soap sold in most parts of Dharavi. This is mainly detergent, used for washing clothes. But the price difference between these local brands and non-brands and those produced by multinationals ensures that the former have a ready market in Dharavi.

Each new wave of migrants has spawned a new trade that has eventually taken root in Dharavi. The latest community of entrepreneurs in Dharavi are the Biharis. No one knows how many there are as no survey has been conducted recently. The 1986 NSDF survey had counted only seventy-five Biharis. Today, they are clearly many more as you find them in every trade, particularly in leather finished goods. The people who complain most bitterly about their arrival are the old Maharashtrian leather workers. 'They (the Biharis) will work for half of what anyone else asks,' said one such worker. 'As a result, we are losing our jobs, and they are coming in.'

Abdul Malik is from Champaran district in Bihar. He came to Dharavi forty years ago for *rozi roti*. Today, this bearded, white-haired man of indeterminate age, has a shop selling handles, zips for suitcases and leather belts which he manufactures in his home. His shop also undertakes repairs of suitcases.

'People in our village used to be amazed at even the name, Bombay,' he says. When he first came to the city, he did a variety of odd jobs. In 1996, he started making suitcases, belts and bags.

Abdul Malik's home is his factory. In the loft, a

group of workers from Bihar are making leather belts. One man can make 100 poor-quality belts or twenty-five high-quality ones in a day. Most of these workers sleep where they work. They get their meals from a *bissi*, which charges them a monthly rate of Rs 550 per person for two meals.

During the riots, many of the Biharis ran away, says Abdul Malik. But they came back once normalcy was restored and also brought back with them more Biharis. The newcomers include young boys. No one knows how many of them are in Dharavi. According to some estimates, there are at least 15,000 Bihari boys working in different workshops in Dharavi. You can find them in every business. Hardly any of them are on the voters' list, admits Malik. So officially they don't exist.

According to some employers, the boys are reportedly willing to work for as little as Rs 500 a year which they send to their parents. They are given a place to live in, food, and are trained in a trade. After two years, they become trained and can earn independently.

Is there a future?

Despite the variety and range of industries and manufacturing units, Dharavi continues to be regarded primarily as a residential area. All plans for its redevelopment centre on housing for its residents without taking into account the fact that people live in Dharavi because they find work there. Despite efforts by NSDF and its partner, Dharavi Vikas Samiti, to press home the point that Dharavi is above all an industrial area, the government refuses to pay heed.

Part of the reason for this is the Mumbai Development Plan which had envisaged decongestion of the island city. This meant not just moving industries out but also denying permission for any new industries to come up.

D.T. Joseph feels that the lack of planning for employment was a serious lacunae in development plans for Mumbai. 'The main thrust, according to me, lies in employment in an urban area. What is the context of urbanization? If you go back in history, urbanization occurs because people come in from the rural area, the economies of scale occur. This means employment is what you must begin with. But if you see any of your urban policies like the Development Plan, there will not be a word on employment.'

After many years of being involved in urban planning, Joseph concludes that the approach to planning in Mumbai was all wrong. It was elitist, particularly with regard to the island city, and did not pay full heed to people's needs. He says, 'Nowadays, I am of the opinion that even for slum redevelopment, you should think of bettering what is available for them. In Dharavi, if people are exporting, manufacturing, doing well, they are actually professional. Now what kind of accommodation is relevant for these professions? Your rules should be such that they should enable them to come out of this on their own.'

In fact, the approach to town planning in India seems still stuck in colonial concepts which are inappropriate in the face of current realities. Thus, you plan for green areas, for schools, dispensaries, but you do not plan for housing for the poor or for employment for the poor. If you move the sources of employment for the poor, such as factories, in effect you are denying them the right to live in certain parts of the city. Therefore, consciously a city is segregated into areas where only the privileged can gain the benefits of serviced areas while the poor are left to fend for themselves in swamps and land not wanted for any other purpose.

Yet, industrial Dharavi has grown and flourished because the State actually benefits indirectly from the illegality of the enterprises in Dharavi. Although many businesses escape taxes because of the nature of the work, they pay much higher indirect taxes to keep going. These are in the form of regular haftas which must be paid to the police, to the municipal corporation staff and often to the local dada. If these businesses were regularized, their outgoings would probably be much lower.

In fact, the city of Mumbai faces a similar situation with hawkers, who occupy many pavements in the city, selling all manner of goods. Most ordinary people appreciate hawkers because they can find cheap goods practically at their doorstep. But the municipal corporation grants licences only to a few of them. The rest are deemed illegal and live in constant fear of municipal vans which swoop down on groups of hawkers, confiscate all their goods, and levy a hefty fine. This is in addition to the daily hafta that hawkers pay to the police and the municipal corporation staff. The various hawkers' associations have been demanding that all of them be issued licences and given areas where they can sell their goods. But the deadlock between the municipality and the hawkers has not been broken. So the legal and illegal hawkers continue to block pavements in Mumbai and nothing changes.

Apart from the issue of legality, this kind of unregulated enterprise is a great waste of talent and entrepreneurship. Furthermore, it is scripting its own redundancy. Take leather finished goods, for instance. Until the technology for leather processing is enhanced to the point that it can match international standards, no amount of craftsmanship by those in the finished goods industry can capitalize on the export market. This is already evident in Dharavi's leather finished goods market. People are underselling each other, selling almost at cost, to recover their investment as the majority are not able to meet the demands and standards of the export market. Instead of fashioning high-quality leather goods, most of the finished goods businesses in Dharavi are making much lower-quality mass market goods like jewellery boxes.

Similarly, the majority of those in ready-made garments are meeting the needs of the local market and not the export market. With garments being given out to such a large number of jobbers, it is virtually impossible to maintain the level of quality control that the markets in the West demand. As a result, the export that does take place is mainly to the Gulf countries where a limited range of garments are in demand. The rest of the garment business deals mainly in shirts sold cheap for a growing population of men employed in the formal or semi-formal sector not just in Mumbai but in small towns across the country.

The margins at which these businesses work

constantly lead to the more skilled workers being forced out of the job market by those who are less skilled but cheaper. In the leather industry, for instance, many Maharashtrian workers, with generations of experience, have now been marginalized. They complain bitterly about the waves of Bihari youth who are being employed at half the wage, and less than half the skill. But as the skill required today is not of a very high level, it does not take long for a new worker to learn it. Thus, the nature of the business also leads to a certain level of redundancy. But unlike the formal sector, where workers are also being laid off as companies prune their workforce in favour of farming out production, these workers have nothing to fall back upon.

The choice before the government is to either recognize Dharavi as an industrial area and regularize some units as small-scale industries or continue to treat the enterprises there as illegal but do nothing to stop them. If it chooses the latter course, more likely given the past record, then the majority of workers in Dharavi will continue to work in cramped, unhygienic conditions with no security of work in the future.

Even if the area is granted the status of a small-scale industrial estate, the existing businesses will have to invest in upgrading their technology. At their present levels of low technology and low skills, they will not be able to manufacture the quality of goods that will earn them the required returns to survive legally. The choice is between scaling up or scaling out.

4

Cops and Robbers

Rafeeq Ellias

'Dharavi was like an independent state, a law unto itself. It was impossible to walk through it, it was so filthy. The common man could not go there because they feared they would be killed. Dharavi was full of criminal activity. Murder used to be an ordinary thing. The sheer sight of Dharavi used to create a fear psychosis,' recalls Y.C. Pawar, who was the deputy commissioner of police (DCP) of Bombay Zone III from 1982 to 1987.

The majority of the middle class living in cities would not be surprised at this description of Dharavi or any other slum area. They believe that the people who live in these insanitary conditions have in their midst thieves, murderers and rapists who make cities unsafe. They presume that slums encourage crime in cities, that they provide a safe haven to criminals.

This is based on the fallacious assumption that while the rest of the residents of a city follow legal norms, live in ordered housing, pay taxes and abide by general rules of orderly behaviour, the very existence of slums is 'illegal' and their presence represents an open violation of law. Therefore, those who have broken the law, by squatting on vacant land, will inevitably continue to break the law.

That some of the most notorious lawbreakers live in the so-called 'orderly' parts of the city is never acknowledged. Nor the fact that the middle class in most cities resort to blatant illegalities, including violating city planning rules, but never get caught because they have ways to circumvent the law.

In recent years, Mumbai has witnessed some celebrated cases of such violations. In 1999, an upmarket restaurant lost a case its owners had fought for fourteen years to continue using a space which violated building by-laws. There are numerous other restaurants in the city that have encroached on pavements, built awnings, and continue to get away with this illegality. One of them was owned by an ex-mayor of Mumbai. A Shiv Sena municipal corporator managed to construct an entire bungalow in Sion without permission. It was eventually demolished by the municipality. But for every one that is caught, there are dozens who get away because of their economic clout.

The media has played a role, too, in perpetuating this image of criminalized slums. People living in slums are routinely called 'encroachers'. Thus, they are rendered non-people, their only image is as breakers of the law. The fact that millions of law-abiding people live in slums because they have no choice, that they pay taxes, formal or informal, that they work and do not live off the State is rarely emphasized in the unidimensional images being projected.

Hindi films have had their share of showing slums as places where slumlords rape and torture impoverished women, extort money from poor and honest men, and spread terror and mayhem should anyone dare cross their path. The police are shown as being utterly helpless in the face of such outlaws. These images, based on partial reality, are projected as the whole of it.

Another problem with these images is that they conflate two aspects of slums—criminality and the safety of ordinary people. These are two separate issues. The first is linked to larger questions of crime, its link to politics, to State policy, to the police. The second has to do with the nature of cities and, within that context, how life is conducted in slum colonies.

Dharavi's criminal history illustrates how an area's criminal profile is linked to larger issues of crime and politics in cities rather than with anything particular pertaining to that area. Thus, the seeds of crime in Dharavi were laid not as the slum settlement grew from the original fishing village but after 1954, when the policy of prohibition of the sale of liquor was implemented in the breach by the very people given the task of enforcing it. And as Y.C. Pawar himself demonstrated, when the law enforcers actually enforced the law, Dharavi's image changed.

People living in Dharavi recall that crime increased during the prohibition era because those breaking the law—the slumlords or the bootleggers—knew that the law enforcement machinery could not touch them. Thus, they could also resort to other crimes within Dharavi and get away with them because they had become larger than life in the eyes of ordinary people.

This is not to suggest that there was no crime in Dharavi before this period. It certainly existed. For instance, the way slumlords consolidated their hold over large tracts of land was a reality that ordinary people had to contend with regardless of the government's policy on liquor. These are the men who became notorious because they had the ability to bend the law—through fair means or foul. They could mark plots on unoccupied land and 'rent' these out to poor people desperate for a place to live. They would then arrange for a common tap for which they would extract more money. As slums grew, the local political parties recognized the power of these dadas to deliver the votes. Thus, lawbreakers and lawmakers came together. This nexus laid the ground for the organized crime that grew and flourished in subsequent years.

Self-policing

But apart from organized crime, the other reality of slums that is often overlooked is that the most crowded areas of a city are usually the safest. It is the empty streets of posh localities that are often the most unsafe. In a slum, there is rarely any part that is not peopled at all hours of the day and night. Even if many people go out of the slum area for work, as many stay at home. They are either working at home, or minding the house. And they are all watching the street. A stranger is immediately spotted because everyone knows everyone else. In such an area, it would require considerable skill to rob a house, or kidnap a person, without several people noticing, and intervening. Unlike middle-class areas, poor people have no qualms about taking the law into their own hands if they apprehend someone harming their neighbour.

Another reason slum areas are safe for the people living in them is the multiple use of space. Within the same area, you have spaces where people eat and sleep, where they work, and where they conduct trade. Every settlement, consisting of narrow lanes converging into one another in an apparently disorderly manner—but with an internal order which the outsider cannot comprehend—has a grocery store, a laundry, a phone booth, a doctor's clinic (unfortunately, most often an unqualified quack), and a chai shop. With lanes that are barely three feet wide, and with this multiplicity of establishments, petty crime is virtually impossible. That is why even today people feel safe enough to leave their doors open in one room as they sit in another room a few doors away.

The very topography of slums militates against routine policing. In its absence, people presume that there must be anarchy. The reality is quite different. Speak to the residents of a settled slum—that is, one that has been in existence for two or three decades—and they will tell you that they have managed their own affairs quite well without the interference of the police. It is true that many settlements have either a dada or a local politician who is the final arbiter of disputes. The Shiv Sena built its base in the slums by setting up shakhas which settled disputes and also acted as informal employment exchanges. Such arrangements necessarily lead to summary justice at times, but quite often routine disputes get settled without involving the police. In fact, in several areas, it is powerful women who play the role of mediators.

Take Amina from Dharavi's Muslim Nagar, for instance. She heads the Mahim Taluka Mahila Wing of the Congress and also likes to project herself as a social worker. Her neighbourhood is typical of the image one has of slums. There is hardly any natural light in the lanes separating rows of houses because people have built lofts that extend upwards and outwards and almost touch the loft on the opposite side. In a group of a dozen houses you will find people of different communities, speaking different languages, eating their own cuisine. Opposite Amina's house, men from Bengal work day and night on their sewing machines, doing intricate machine embroidery for the local market. In a corner, one of them fries fish for the workers. The smell chokes even those sitting in Amina's house across the lane. On her doorstep, undeterred by the constant passage of people in the lane, sit four children playing carrom.

In the midst of all this activity, Amina conducts an informal counselling and mediation centre. Spend a few hours in one of her rooms—she has several rooms in Muslim Nagar—and you will see the whole panoply of disputes being landed at her doorstep. A woman comes in and complains about her drunkard son who is in trouble with the police, a man asks her to intervene with the municipal corporation on a matter. Amina ticks off the mother for spoiling her son and assures the man that she will try and help.

Many settlements in Dharavi have similar systems. Others like the Kumbhars or the Valmikis have their own jamaats which intervene in disputes. Amongst the Adi Dravidas, their society office is the place where differences between members of the community are brought for mediation and settlement.

In Dharavi, as elsewhere in the city, poor people have a purely pragmatic approach towards the police—or any other authority, like the municipality. They know from experience that anything can be arranged in exchange for money. Thus, paying off the police is the norm; turning to them for help is an exception. In fact, this is not very different from the attitude of people living in middle-class colonies.

At the same time, a growing awareness of rights has made women turn to the police in cases of domestic violence. Social workers are constantly being approached to help women to register non-cognizable offences against their husbands in cases of domestic violence. One social worker says that she cannot convince the women that this in itself will not result in prosecution.

The story of Varda

In the past, Dharavi's crime profile was inextricably linked with liquor. Its marshy conditions made it the ideal ground for brewing illicit liquor. What had been a traditional occupation of the Kolis became big business once the government decided to prohibit the manufacture and sale of alcohol in 1954. 'Country', as the illicit brew was called, ostensibly went underground. In fact, as Dharavi residents will tell you even today, it was brewed openly, in full view of the police and the municipal authorities. Everyone was 'taken care of', as the Kolis candidly admit. And hundreds of litres of 'country' travelled from Dharavi to liquor dens in Mumbai every day despite the ban.

The Kolis, who were traditional brewers of country liquor and still continue to brew, albeit on a much smaller scale, allege that all the problems began when the 'Madrasis' entered the trade and used dubious methods to make the traditional fruit-based brew more potent. They are referring to Tamil migrants who settled in Dharavi to work in tanneries but also turned to brewing illicit liquor at the height of the prohibition era when a great deal of money could be made in the trade. Adulteration of the country liquor with additives like battery cells to increase its potency resulted in deaths. This, insist the Kolis, gave the whole business a bad name. 'Once these people got into it, the reputation of country as adulterated brew got around and our business was affected,' says one of the Kolis.

The most famous, or infamous, of these 'Madrasis' was Vardarajan Mudaliar, or Varda. The kingpin of the liquor mafia that grew out of the prohibition era, Varda operated out of Dharavi's Koliwada and lived in Matunga. There are many legends and myths that have grown around Varda. He was admired and feared. His was one of the biggest gangs. The police crackdown on the Varda gang gave Mumbai the image of being the centre of gangland and Dharavi as the centre of all criminal activity.

Old residents of Dharavi, like Khatija from Kasargode, will tell you, 'I remember in those days, as soon as it became dark, people were afraid to move around. Taxis would not come to Dharavi because there had been many murders. People were hacked to death with the *koiti* (sword). If you had a little gold or money, you were targeted by the dadas. You either gave them what they wanted, or you were dead.'

But the fights were mostly between the various gangs and ordinary people were generally left untouched. In fact, women like Amina fault the prohibition policy for the problems Dharavi faced. 'Everything was fine in Dharavi until prohibition came. Before that, there used to be scores of liquor stills employing many people. There were no fights, no crime. We never had doors on our huts, only curtains. Once prohibition came, and the liquor business was stopped, the problems started. People were put out of work, and that is when Dharavi changed. Fights began to take place.' Prohibition did not really stop liquor brewing; it merely made it illegal and raised the price. As the Kolis and the police confirm, brewing continued openly in Dharavi well into the 1980s.

Amina acknowledges, however, that women did face problems from the dadas who ran the liquor business. '*Bahut paap hota tha*,' she says. 'They would just take any woman they fancied and no one would dare raise an objection. The police were paid off, so they would not listen to any complaints. So many young girls were made pregnant by these men and then abandoned. Most of these girls left Dharavi and went back to their villages.'

Khatija and Amina have a dramatic turn of phrase, as do many people in Dharavi. But they do not exaggerate, confirms Y.C. Pawar, the policeman credited with getting rid of the Varda gang from Bombay.

Pawar was the DCP of Bombay Zone III, which includes Dharavi, from June 1982 to January 1987. This was the period that Vardarajan's gang ruled over large parts of Bombay. Its main business was illicit liquor. Much of this was manufactured in Dharavi. The local inspectors were either bought out or scared out of their wits, according to Pawar. Either way they did nothing to stop the business which flourished right through the period when liquor was supposed to be prohibited in Bombay.

Pawar was brought into the job by Julio F. Ribeiro, who came in as Bombay's commissioner of police. Ribeiro had known what Dharavi was like during an earlier spell when he was a DCP. 'I was deputy commissioner from 1969 to 1972,' he recalls, 'and Dharavi was always a difficult place. All the illegal activity used to flourish there—liquor and gambling. Middle-class people would not go there.' Over this period, Ribeiro took on the task of cleaning up Dharavi. 'We swept all the marshes. The whole place was full of illicit liquor stills.' His regular policemen did not want to go there. So Ribeiro decided to use new recruits from the Police Training School in Marol. Once a week they were sent to wade through the swamp and to smash the stills. He says these systematic raids on the distilleries convinced people that the police were serious about implementing the law.

When Ribeiro was appointed commissioner of police in 1982, he realized that there was one man who could deal with the growing hold of the Varda gang in Bombay, and that was Y.C. Pawar. At Ribeiro's behest, Pawar was appointed DCP of Bombay Zone III.

Soon after he took office, Pawar made the Varda problem his priority. He first targeted the illicit liquor distilleries in Dharavi and had many of them smashed. They had reappeared after the earlier effort at ending the illicit liquor business. Of this period, Ribeiro writes in his book *Bullet for Bullet*: 'After Y.C. Pawar took over as DCP, Zone III, the most notorious distilleries in the Sion creek, which had doubled in recent days, were totally eliminated. The people who passed by that creek every day were used to seeing the fires that indicated the presence of these distilleries. They were totally amazed at the transformation. They had earlier been told that eliminating the distilleries was not possible because of the inhospitable terrain. Now they realized that successive officers had merely tried to hoodwink them while actually conniving at the illegal activities.'

Having tackled the liquor stills, Pawar took on the delivery system which was managed by Thomas Kurien alias Khaja, Varda's right-hand man. Every day, hundreds of taxis would leave his shop in Antop Hill carrying liquor. Pawar estimates that 10,000-20,000 litres of illicit liquor was manufactured and distributed every day. The main mode of transport was taxis. Pawar's efforts at tracking down Khaja paid off when, after a dramatic forty-minute chase, he managed to intercept Khaja and arrest him. This was the first message to Varda that the police were on to him.

In 1985, the police managed to file a case of attempted murder against Varda and he was arrested for a day and kept in the police lock-up. A year later 'Tillu', alias Darshankumar Santram Dhalla, another of Varda's lieutenants, was picked up and Varda was also implicated in the case. This is when Varda realized that he was in trouble, says Pawar, and escaped to Chennai.

The Bombay police declared Mudaliar Vardarajan an absconder. But only one of his properties could be attached as he had made sure that all the rest were benami. This, however, effectively ensured that Varda could not return to Bombay and with two of his right-hand men behind bars, his gang was broken. Varda died some years later in Chennai.

Pawar was given an award for this effort in 1986. But he had also stepped on the toes of the political establishment. So even as he was decorated, he was transferred to Nanded by S.B. Chavan, who was the chief minister at that time.

Pawar says that it was only when the police succeeded in breaking the back of the main gang operating in the area did Dharavi's development proceed. 'Otherwise even the government machinery could not go there,' he says.

Identity politics

Although gang warfare ended in Dharavi with the end of the Varda gang, the problems of policing the area did not. A new set of problems cropped up with the spread of identity politics. Dharavi, like other slums, is an ideal breeding ground for this brand of politics. Ordinarily, people of all communities have to summon up their reserves of tolerance for each other because, given the proximity within which people live in mixed localities, there is no option. But for every mixed neighbourhood, there are dozens of exclusive settlements where people of only one community live. It is here that the seeds of suspicion against another community can be sown, and later harvested.

As Dharavi grew, the Kolis felt greatly outnumbered. Today, they constitute only 6 per cent of the population of Dharavi. As a result, when the Shiv Sena came around in the late 1960s with its propaganda of the rights of sons of the soil, it found a ready response amongst the Kolis. They responded to the party in 1966-67, when its anti-south Indian propaganda triggered off riots in Bombay, for by then the Tamilians of Dharavi had become their economic rivals in the liquor trade.

But as the nature of Shiv Sena's politics shifted from anti-outsider to anti-Muslim, the Kolis too made the switch. Old friendships with the Muslim boys down Dharavi Main Road notwithstanding, people who had lived amicably along Dharavi Main Road were divided right down the centre. Ironically, the 'Madrasis', the old rivals of the Kolis, ultimately came on their side in the Hindu-Muslim divide. Although few Tamilians joined the Sena, many more responded to the Hindutva call of the Bharatiya Janata Party (BJP). Thus, when the Babri Masjid was demolished on 6 December 1992, the battle lines were already drawn in Dharavi.

Never before had the police faced such a challenge in Dharavi as during the 1992-93 riots. They were caught completely unprepared for the explosion of anger that took place on 6 December when the Shiv Sena led a cycle rally, celebrating the demolition of the Babri Masjid, right through the heart of the Muslim neighbourhoods. In fact, the police should have been alert to the possibility of a conflagration between Hindus and Muslims as the Shiv Sena and the BJP had increased the tempo of their campaign for the Ram Temple in Ayodhya from as far back as 1989. Although no major clash had taken place in the preceding two years, tension was evident and all it required was a small spark.

I saw first-hand how easy it was to start a riot in Dharavi. This was in early January, when Bombay had barely recovered from the vicious rioting that followed the demolition of the Babri Masjid. Many localities, including Dharavi, had been under curfew. The death toll in the first phase of rioting, which began on 6 December and continued until 16 December, was 227 with many injured. Fear had gripped many parts of a city which had not seen such a riot in many decades. The government appeared unprepared to deal with what was happening on the streets.

For a couple of weeks, from the end of December to early January, curfew was lifted and the city appeared to be limping back to normal. But the peace began to break down again on 5 January, when reports filtered in that two Mathadi workers (loaders in the docks) had been stabbed. Even before it could be ascertained who had stabbed them, the rumour mills began spreading the story that they had been killed by Muslims.

The very next day, rioting broke out again in many parts of the city. In Dharavi, sword-wielding Hindus attacked Muslim areas. Prominent local Shiv Sena leaders, many of them Kolis, were reported to be participants in this. Homes, shops and factories were set on fire, godowns were looted. Once again curfew was clamped over Dharavi and other precincts of the city.

On 8 January, a Friday, the police decided to lift curfew in Dharavi for a few hours to permit Muslims to attend Friday prayers at the local mosque. Until then, assembly of more that five people had been prohibited. I went to Dharavi to check whether things were returning to normal. Unbeknownst to me, and to the rest of

Dharavi, a huge storm was just waiting to break over the city as in the early hours of that very morning, a Hindu family had been burned alive in their home in East Jogeshwari, a large slum in the north-eastern suburb of Bombay. News about this was just getting around the city and word had gone out to the Shiv Sena cadres to 'teach them', meaning the Muslims, 'a lesson'. But at that hour of the morning, the news had not yet reached most of Dharavi.

On normal days, Dharavi Main Road—an euphemism for a pitted, narrow track—is virtually impassable. Once it must have been the 'main' road. Today, it is narrow and crowded, a lane pretending to be a road, with shops on either side that have encroached and ruined any chance of alignment. The space that is left is half taken on either side by street hawkers. Somehow, in between all this, people, animals, bicyclists, two-wheelers, autorickshaws, taxis, private cars, tempos, mini-trucks all jostle for space. There is potential for a full-scale riot every single day. But it does not happen.

On that winter day of 8 January 1993, the road was deserted despite the lifting of curfew. A few people cautiously stepped out, looked around. A couple of hawkers bravely started vending their wares. And Muslim men, dressed in white, began making their way to Dharavi's oldest mosque, the Badi Masjid, located at the halfway point of Dharavi Main Road.

We sat in Shafi Building, right next to Badi Masjid, talking to a group of people about the riots. Shafi Building was the first multi-storeyed building to come up in Dharavi. It is built on private land and is three storeys high. Today, it is dwarfed by higher structures but remains a local landmark.

Even as we asked people about the days of rioting, we heard a commotion outside. From that height we got a clear view of the road. To our left was Badi Masjid. The namaazis were emerging from the mosque. In a split second, we saw some of the younger men dart into the lanes on the other side of the road. I also noticed that there were piles of loose bricks conveniently lying at different points of the road. Within minutes, these bricks were being passed around.

The rows of low-rise buildings of Chamda Bazaar across the mosque were the battlefield. On both sides, young men on different sides of the dividing line climbed the roofs. They used metal *palats* (trays used by construction workers to carry bricks and cement) as their shields. Their weapons were bricks and bottles, which also appeared as if out of nowhere.

The battle began. Missiles from one side flew, the other side ducked. Then the other side flung missiles, and the first lot ducked. For ten minutes, the battle continued. But as quickly as it had begun, it subsided with the sound of the first police siren. The vans arrived, the blue-uniformed policemen jumped out and ran through the lanes waving lathis and firing guns.

In less than half an hour, the 'riot' had ended. Three people had died; many had been injured; the pretence of 'normalcy' had been shattered. The two warring sides were Muslims and the Kolis (Hindu fisherfolk)—different religions, different political loyalties. We learnt later that Koli women had taken out a protest morcha because they objected to the lifting of the curfew for the Friday prayers. As the morcha approached Badi Masjid, some young men began pelting stones in the direction of the mosque. This triggered off the riot.

This mini-riot illustrates the problem of policing slums in normal times or during times of communal tension. When communities are already polarized, it takes little to spark off a riot. In normal times, it could be something as innocuous as a ball breaking a window pane during a gully cricket match. The very geography of slums seems to facilitate rooftop battles which lead to casualties at the ground level. And by the time the police arrive, it is often too late. No intelligence network can alert the police about such outbreaks of violence.

DCP saheb

This then is the Dharavi that the police had to confront during the 1992-93 riots, a place that was like a tinderbox. A name often mentioned by people in Dharavi is 'Pandey saheb'. They are referring to a young police officer who was posted as the DCP at Dharavi during the entire period of the riots. Sanjay Pandey established a reputation as a tough but fair cop. He was seen to be even-handed in one of the most communally-sensitive localities of the city. And his personal involvement won the trust of many ordinary people. For instance, at the height of the riots, he would spend the night at the Dharavi police station, which is located halfway down 90 Feet Road and literally in the middle of the settlement.

One of the first major incidents during the weeks of the riots took place in Dharavi on 6 December, soon after news of the demolition of the Babri Masjid reached the people. It was triggered off by the Shiv Sena's cycle rally celebrating the demolition. It appears that the party did not seek permission for the rally. The procession went through the most sensitive parts of Dharavi.

The Justice B.N. Srikrishna Commission, which was set up by the Maharashtra government on 25 January 1993 to look into the causes of the riots, came down heavily on the police for its inaction in this instance. 'This cycle rally was nothing but an attempt by the Shiv Sena to provoke Muslims by rubbing salt in their wounds by open gloating over what was, from the point of view of the Muslims, an unfortunate and tragic event. The consequences of permitting such a procession ought to have been foreseen by any police officer worth his salt. The police are to be squarely blamed for this unpardonable act. What transpired thereafter bears out this conclusion,' stated the report of the commission, which was released only on 16 February 1998.

The cycle rally inevitably triggered off a response from the Muslims, who first took out a peaceful procession in protest. But confronted with hostile groups, who threw stones at the procession, and an insensitive police which charged with batons at the processionists, they lost their cool and went on the rampage. Thus, in the course of a few hours, Dharavi was turned into a communal cauldron. Each side attacked the other; religious places were the main targets, but so were the businesses. Thus, Chamda Bazaar, which had many small Muslim-owned workshops doing jobwork for garment exporters and some shops with finished leather goods, was razed to the ground.

That things had gone completely out of hand in

Dharavi during the first two days of the riots was evident. It was at this juncture that Sanjay Pandey was posted to Dharavi.

To catch the main troublemakers in this situation was no easy task. A tough policeman could easily have been accused of favouring one side or the other. The potential for such misunderstanding was even greater because numerically the Hindus and Muslims are almost equal in Dharavi.

Furthermore, the period of the riots had clearly revealed that the beat cop was imbued with deep inbuilt prejudices that came into play during times of trouble. The Mumbai police, once considered the best in the country, was strongly indicted by the Srikrishna Commission. Repeatedly, Justice B.N. Srikrishna noted the biased attitude of the police: 'The Commission is of the view that there is evidence of police bias against Muslims which has manifested itself in other ways like the harsh treatment given to them, failure to register even cognizable offences by Muslim complainants . . . That there was a general bias against the Muslims in the minds of the average policeman which was evident in the way they dealt with the Muslims, is accepted by the officer of the rank of Additional Commissioner, V.N. Deshmukh.'

In another part of the report the judge notes: 'The response of police to appeals from desperate victims, particularly Muslims, was cynical and utterly indifferent. On occasions, the response was that they were unable to leave the appointed post; on others, the attitude was that one Muslim killed, was one Muslim less.'

In such a situation, where the constabulary is biased,

how should a senior police officer conduct his affairs and ensure that all the communities, specially the minorities, have confidence in the police?

Sanjay Pandey says that he had a simple formula for dealing with both crime and the communal problem. 'If you catch the highest criminal, everything else falls into place,' he says. Too often, he says, the police catch the small fish and let the big fish go scot-free. 'In Dharavi, we decided to work the other way round.'

Indeed, the Srikrishna Commission commended the officer for moving swiftly in one case where a complainant, a Muslim, had repeatedly asked the help of the police to remove the Shiv Sena activists who had forcibly occupied his premises. Pandey took immediate action. The commission noted: 'It is obvious to the Commission that the police at the lower levels were under the strong influence of Shiv Sena hoodlums and there was at least one straight-forward officer who promptly responded to the complainant and took quick and decisive action.'

Pandey says that he realized early on that he could not police Dharavi by patrolling or by fixed pickets. Instead, he had to understand the internal dynamics of the settlements and operate accordingly. This is easier said than done, given the density of the settlements. Residents of Dharavi recount incidents of policemen running through their settlements without a clue as to where they were headed. Their task was rendered virtually impossible without support from the local people. In those tightly knit areas, you can spend hours walking around without knowing where you are going to come out. If the person trying to escape the police decides to hide in one of these settlements, it is impossible to trace him.

Pandey divided Dharavi into several areas. He realized that each pocket had its own strongman. He collected this information from people. Sometimes the person was a criminal, sometimes a politician, and sometimes these roles were combined. He felt he had to locate this kingpin before he could move.

Although Pandey was unable to take any action against the supposed ringleaders during the riots, where just putting out the fires kept the entire force on its toes, he was able to implement the policy when peace returned. He claims that once the leaders had been identified and arrested, even if in some cases a clear connection between the crime and the leader could not be established, incidents of crime came down.

Mohalla Committees

People in Dharavi had their own response to the riots. Despite the exemplary work of individuals like Pandey, there was a general loss of faith in the police after the riots. While the riots were still on, an informal group of Hindus and Muslims came together in Dharavi to form a Mohalla Committee to provide relief to riot victims. They had to deal with displacement as entire neighbourhoods emptied out in fear, with people who had lost their businesses, with families who had to deal with the death of a loved one in police firing or in the violent clashes between Hindus and Muslims. With the aid of the larger citizens' peace effort that was working in the rest of the city, the Dharavi group tried to help with the immediate crisis.

Women like Amina, who was a member of the Mohalla Committee but has subsequently stepped down, have amazing stories to tell about those days. When the violence was at its peak, Amina was one of the few people to come out of her settlement to see if she could do anything to help.

Some of her stories are both dramatic and terrifying. The most interesting was how the women in Muslim Nagar solved the problems of a shortage of *kafans*. When two young men from Muslim Nagar were killed in police firing, they could not get shrouds in which to wrap the bodies. Amina's Hindu women friends, Hira and Kamala, offered to go out and get them. Despite the curfew and the dangers of stepping out of the settlement, they made their way to the Mahim mosque by saying they were Hindus when they went through Hindu areas, and pretending they were Muslims in Muslim areas. Finally, when they reached the mosque, the maulvi was suspicious and insisted on calling Amina to check if she had sent these women. He used the Muslim names that they had given him. For a moment Amina forgot that Kamala and Hira had gone on her behalf and almost denied knowing them. Fortunately, she remembered that they would adopt Muslim names and reassured the maulvi that she had sent the two women.

Although Hindu-Muslim clashes were taking place all over Dharavi, Amina and her group of women managed to keep the peace in their part of the settlement. 'We told people that we must stick together and then neither Muslim nor Hindu would be affected,' she says.

People in Dharavi, as elsewhere in Mumbai, took it

upon themselves to guard their settlements from attacks because they had little faith in the police. Nightly vigils were kept in many areas. The women took on the task of keeping the men awake by supplying them with tea through the night. One such woman was Mariam Rashid, who heads the Society for Human and Environmental Development (SHED) programme in Dharavi.

Recalling those days, she says: 'I was a social worker even before the riots. I used to live in a house in Kamala Nehru Nagar, a mixed neighbourhood of around 250 to 300 families, with my husband and daughter as well as his two brothers. One day a whole bunch of Tamilians came to our settlement with the specific intent of attacking me. They had seen me organizing the nightly watch. The men would stay up all night and I would provide them with tea so that they would remain awake. I was seen as the main organizer of this. So they targeted me. No one dared approach our settlement at night. So they tried during the day. I had to go out and literally force the men to come out and confront these men. When they hesitated, I threatened them saying that I would let these Tamil boys loot their houses if they did not come out.'

As a result of her haranguing them, the men did come out and the attackers ran away. But in a few days, practically the entire settlement emptied out. All the families, Hindus and Muslims, moved away to other areas because, according to Mariam, 'they saw my presence there as a danger'. Mariam herself refused to leave and 'luckily for me my husband decided to stay. But my brothers-in-law also left. We became far more vulnerable as a result of this.' With hindsight, she now wonders whether she should have cared so much about the rest of them. 'Perhaps I should have just thought of the safety of my own family and left the settlement when I realized I was being targeted,' she says.

Despite these experiences during the riots, Mariam remains an active member of Dharavi's Mohalla Committee which was formalized after the riots. Since then, it has spread to other parts of the city. Mohalla Committees have members of the community and representatives of the police. People with political affiliations are not allowed to be members. Hence, Amina had to step down.

Dharavi's Mohalla Committee set an example for other such committees that were formed in the most troubled neighbourhoods of Mumbai. Although today many of them also tackle other needs, like cleaning up their areas, or providing recreation facilities for young people, their main concern remains creating and maintaining communal harmony.

Each year, during the Ganesh Festival, the Dharavi Mohalla Committee is particularly active. In the past, there would always be tension because the Kolis would insist on taking their procession past the Badi Masjid on Dharavi Main Road. Often, there were minor incidents when the two communities would clash. Nowadays, the maulvis of the mosque actually welcome the procession and provide water to the processionists. In return, the Hindus have agreed to tone down the music during their festivals in the Muslim-majority areas, particularly during times when they are at prayer. In fact, members of all the communities have sat down and arrived at an agreed set of rules for festivals to minimize chances of clashes between different groups.

J.F. Ribeiro, who since his retirement lives in Mumbai and has been closely associated with the Mohalla Committees in the city, is convinced that in the long run, the only way to police areas like Dharavi is through community policing as demonstrated by the work of the Mohalla Committee.

Crime and poverty

Now that the riots are receding in people's memories, and the days of Varda and his gang are even further back, is Dharavi still a stronghold of criminals?

According to Pandey, most of the criminals in Dharavi are 'need-based' criminals.

Dharavi's bad name, he says, comes from people caught for crimes in other parts of Mumbai who have links with the place or live there. For example, many small-time pickpocket gangs working the suburban trains report to people who operate out of Dharavi. But Pandey acknowledges that Dharavi provides the manpower for gangsters. The main recruits for the criminal gangs are the increasing number of youngsters born and brought up in Dharavi who know no other life, he says. Many of them have no education, they hang around on the street and are ready to join these gangs.

Amina confirms this. She says, 'Amongst us Muslims, we still don't send our children to school. If they fail after the third or the fourth, we pull them out and send them to work in a garage or somewhere else. The young boys become goondas. What else can they do? We marry the girls off early because it's too risky otherwise.' The recruits for the gangs are not restricted to any one community. Many of the Hindu boys who are part of the Shiv Sena's shakhas are also known to be part of local gangs.

The legacy of the riots has also contributed to the increase in crime and violent incidents. Apart from minor riots that seem to get sparked off for almost no reason, there has been a gradual change in the population profile in many settlements. As in Naya Chawl, Palwadi, Hindus or Muslims who felt insecure in their particular part of Dharavi have moved elsewhere or moved out altogether. Other people have moved in, people who have no relationship with their neighbours. Also, with Dharavi's now more important location, and the subsequent rise in property prices, many families have sold their houses and moved either to a newer settlement in Dharavi or out of Dharavi. Thus, the cohesiveness of the past is already beginning to break down. Inevitably, this will result in more clashes than in the past.

Amina and other women also talk of the increase in liquor bars and dancing bars in Dharavi. After the riots, a group of women had gone around demanding the closure of these bars because they insisted that they corrupted their youth and also brought in strangers into Dharavi who harassed young women.

For a while, the campaign worked. But before long the bars reappeared and are now prominent in many parts of the settlement. Inevitably, the changes that the rest of the city of Mumbai is witnessing are finding an echo in settlements like Dharavi.

These changes suggest that the police has to rethink

how it polices these areas rather than sticking to its old, dysfunctional methods. Both Pandey and Ribeiro have a similar approach to policing slums. Says Ribeiro, 'Dharavi needs to be policed with the help of the people. They have to cooperate. Even if the police can do more than what they are doing now, they won't because most of such areas are very lucrative for the police. Even if there are poor people, there's quantity. The scales are vast.'

In fact, it is the moneymaking aspect of policing that continuously undercuts any confidence-building exercise that individual police officers or groups like the Mohalla Committee might attempt between people and the police. Slum upgradation policies, for instance, have led to another avenue for collection for the police. People in Dharavi say that even if you are seen carrying a bag of cement to undertake minor repairs in your house, the police will be at your doorstep demanding payment. If you do not pay up, you are booked under Section 151 of the Indian Penal Code for which you can be detained for twenty-four hours.

According to Ribeiro, 'The police who are in charge would normally get involved in the money generating activities. It's not easy in a totally slum area. They form a partnership with the criminals. Officers who really want to do something have to form a partnership with the people against the criminals. If the people find that the police are on their side, they would participate. But the problem is that they see that the police are on the side of the criminals.'

This statement perhaps sums up best the basic issue of crime and poor people in a city like Mumbai or for that matter any other city. The nexus between criminals, politicians and the police is so open that ordinary people have lost faith in the system. They turn to their own systems of protection and justice—to save them from the official system which, they assume, will victimize them because they are poor.

Poor people also constantly witness how the police justifies its existence by picking on easy targets, often the lowest in the chain, who would be a poor person turning to low-level crime for survival, while the kingpins of the criminal trade escape untouched. The liquor trade flourished during the prohibition era because, as the Kolis state, the police and the politicians 'were taken care of'. If anyone was caught, it would be a poor man transporting liquor from the stills to taxis or godowns.

Furthermore, if the State itself endorses lawlessness by permitting the breaking of the law, it is laughable to talk about enforcing the rule of law. Places like Dharavi become criminalized precisely because of this, and not because poor people have a criminal mentality. As long as the law is enforced in an unequal manner, crime will not be checked.

5

A House for Khatija

Ayesha Taleyarkhan

Khatija lives in the Dargah Chawl of Dharavi's Social Nagar. Today, her house is typical of the incrementally improved structures you see around you. But just thirty years ago, it was just thatch and bamboo. 'When we came here, there must have been hardly 5,000 people. It was all jungle. There was tall grass all around. There were snakes. We built the house with bamboo poles and chatai. It had to be replaced after each monsoon. I brought sacks of mud and filled this place,' recalls Khatija.

Now her house is made of brick and concrete. It has a phone, a TV, a fridge and a washing machine—the latter she says she uses very occasionally. All the crockery is arranged neatly on a shelf on the wall of her spacious front room. There are two beds in the room, a couple of chairs, a table and a sewing machine. The kitchen is located in a room at the back and like most others in Dharavi, Khatija too has a loft the same size as her front room. She does not have piped water inside the house but a tap is located conveniently just outside the house. Khatija has a separate electric meter and proudly shows me her bimonthly bill for Rs 371.

When people like Khatija first came to live in Dharavi, they had no electricity; now they have electric meters. For years they had to share community taps; now many of them have taps in their homes. For years the open fields were the only toilets; today, there are municipal toilets, albeit unusable on many days. Many things have changed, but much also remains unchanged.

There were two concurrent developments that marked the beginning of Dharavi's transformation from a slum on a swamp to a settlement with a mixture of low-rise pucca houses like Khatija's and high-rise buildings built by the government and private builders. Both took place because as Mumbai expanded, Dharavi's location shifted from being at one end of the island city to almost the centre of Mumbai.

The first was a determined effort by the police to tackle crime and the criminal gangs that worked out of Dharavi. This brought about a change of attitude in the general public towards a place that was considered dangerous. It also allowed normal development work to proceed, something that reportedly could not be done earlier because of the criminal activity centred in and around Dharavi.

The second development took place in December 1985 when the Congress' centenary celebrations were held in Bombay. On this occasion, Rajiv Gandhi, who had been elected Prime Minister following the assassination of his mother, Indira Gandhi, in 1984, visited the city. He was taken on a tour of Dharavi and some other slums.

Rajiv Gandhi was moved by what he saw and announced that the Central government would release Rs 100 crore for slum redevelopment and other projects to improve life for the urban poor in Bombay. The scheme was christened the Prime Minister's Grant Project (PMGP).

The grant, however, was not the consequence of

sudden magnanimity. It grew out of the realization that Dharavi was ideally located and that its development would be profitable in many different ways.

D.T. Joseph confirms that the magnanimity towards Dharavi was not accidental. 'In the case of Dharavi, location becomes extremely important. In the sixties and seventies, they may not have realized but by early eighties they would have realized that they were sitting on a gold mine.'

How valuable was the real estate in Dharavi would only emerge in the early 1990s when the concept of developing a new business district across the Mahim creek was touted. This thinking coincided with the opening up of the Indian economy, with expectations that Mumbai would emerge as an important financial centre. It also led to a boom in property prices. Dharavi's location close to these new planned developments elevated its property status.

On receiving the Rs 100 crore grant from the Centre, the state government had to decide how to tackle Dharavi for the PMGP. In 1986, it commissioned a leading architect, Charles Correa, to head a committee which was asked to prepare a report on how Dharavi should be redeveloped. The committee began with a major handicap. It did not have data as no systematic survey of the structures and settlements that made up Dharavi had ever been done.

Rather than go through the painstaking and slow task of an actual physical enumeration, the Correa Committee and the government asked the Hyderabad-based National Remote Sensing Agency to do an aerial survey of Dharavi. It is not surprising, therefore, that the numbers they arrived at—of an estimated population of 2.5 lakh—were so far off the mark as more detailed surveys later proved. For given the way houses are laid out in Dharavi, with lanes merging into each other in a crazy and unplanned manner, it would require some extraordinarily high precision cameras to identify where one house ends and another begins.

Despite this inadequate data, the Correa Committee made some useful suggestions. It pinpointed the inadequacy of infrastructure, such as storm-water drains, as one of the main problems facing Dharavi. As a result, large parts of Dharavi would be flooded during the rains. Also, the water supply was far from adequate because the water mains, bringing in treated water into the city, did not extend to this area. And there was no underground sewerage system and practically no garbage collection. The committee also noted the huge shortage of toilets in Dharavi and stated that even where toilets had been built by the municipality, they were poorly maintained. According to one survey, there were 800 people using one toilet in Dharavi.

The Correa Committee recognized that although the structures in which people lived were unsatisfactory, they had not tried to improve them because they lacked a legal title to the land. Furthermore, existing regulations prevented them from making any substantial improvements in their homes. For instance, people were not permitted to build a loft. Any change in the structure required permission from the local authorities. This gave petty officials the power to extort money from poor people already strapped for resources.

On the positive side, the report recognized that

people in Dharavi were engaged in gainful economic activities that were useful for the rest of the city and that people were genuinely interested in improving their settlements. The committee suggested that given these facts, the problem could be tackled at two broad levels. One was at the area level where deficiencies in infrastructure could be tackled by the government. The second was at the block level where communities would be encouraged to form cooperative societies with about 100 to 150 members who could undertake upgradation if the state gave them land tenure, finance and related services. 'Given the enthusiasm of the residents for undertaking upgradation, if land tenure and finance are provided, the problems of shelter and related services can be solved,' stated the report.

These concepts were acceptable to people living in Dharavi. What was not so acceptable was the idea mooted in the Correa report of accommodating only 43,000 households out of an estimated 55,000—a figure that was at best a guesstimate—and shifting the rest so that there would be adequate open spaces for parks and other recreational facilities. Those that would have to be shifted included households living under high-tension power lines, close to railway tracks and alongside roads that needed to be widened. To minimize the inconvenience to these families, the Correa Committee recommended that land be located close to Dharavi for relocation.

The committee also suggested that all tanneries in Dharavi be shifted to Deonar in north-east Mumbai, thereby locating them closer to the abattoir. Relocating tanneries would free twenty-one acres which could be used for other purposes.

Another important concept articulated by the Correa Committee was the need to set up a separate planning authority to deal with the redevelopment of Dharavi. Many plans had been tied up in bureaucratic knots because of the multiplicity of institutions dealing with questions of slum redevelopment and housing. For instance, land comes under the respective owner of the land on which a slum is located—the Central government, the state government, the railways, the airports authority, the municipal corporation or private owners. The planning needs of the area come under the Maharashtra Housing and Area Development Authority (MHADA). In addition, the municipal corporation has certain powers and policies and the state government has another set. There is often an overlap between these different bodies which holds up implementation of schemes. One authority for slum redevelopment would simplify matters and accelerate implementation. This suggestion laid the grounds for the PMGP scheme which followed.

Prime Minister's Grant Project

At that time, a young IAS officer was posted to Mumbai after the mandatory stint in the districts. Gautam Chatterjee found himself placed in the unenviable position of having to devise a way to spend the Rs 100 crore that had come to Mumbai, and specifically how to use this in Dharavi.

'Dharavi then used to stink. Even my driver would complain. Because this is a place where everything is recycled, animal waste, human waste, everything,' recalls Chatterjee. Of course, not all the money came to Dharavi. Inevitably, there was heavy bargaining from different interest groups. 'People asked why the entire amount should be given to Dharavi,' says Chatterjee. 'There was a pro- and anti-Dharavi group. It was argued that the major problem in Mumbai is not slums but the old dilapidated buildings. Rs 41 crore went for reconstruction of old dilapidated tenanted buildings. After deducting the Rs 37 crore for Dharavi, the remaining was for slum upgradation in the rest of Mumbai.' But even Rs 37 crore was a generous amount, the kind of money that had never been invested in Dharavi before.

Up to the mid-1980s, the government's approach to slums had changed progressively. In the 1960s and early 1970s, its only policy was slum removal, sending in bulldozers or squads to demolish slums. Such an approach had proved politically damaging to the ruling Congress, particularly in the mid-1970s. In north India, the policy had actually led to a noticeable decrease in its vote. Before this, the party had projected itself as a party of the poor, including the urban poor, under Mrs Indira Gandhi's populist slogan of 'Garibi Hatao'. The policy of demolitions, on the other hand, was seen as a policy to remove the poor.

Electoral reversals and other factors led to some rethinking and the subsequent policy of slum improvement and later slum upgradation. These policies recognized that people who came into the city to work would squat on vacant land if there was no affordable housing available to them. It would be futile to chase them away. Therefore, it was more prudent to recognize their existence, and provide them with basic amenities.

The Maharashtra government's slum improvement

scheme was launched after the government conducted a slum census in 1976—which on most counts was inadequate as it left out large sections of urban poor like pavement dwellers. For the first time, there was a number to show how many people lived in slums. Households that were counted in the census were issued a photopass and these slums were then 'recognized' and provided basic services like metered electrical connections and adequate number of community standposts for water and toilets. But slum-dwellers were still not granted tenure and were under the threat of being evicted at any point when the land on which they lived was needed for another purpose. The photopass, however, assured them an alternative site if they were asked to move.

The government census created two classes of slum-dwellers—those with a photopass and those without. Thousands of families who had lived for decades on pavements, along railway tracks, on airport land, were not counted and therefore were not 'recognized'. They continued to live under constant threat of eviction.

In the 1980s, the government went a step beyond slum improvement. It launched the slum upgradation scheme. This had two components. The first permitted slum-dwellers to improve their existing structures *in situ*. It allowed them to raise the height of their huts by building a loft or mezzanine. The basic services, of water and toilets, were further improved. The government also took on the task to pave the lanes between the houses and to provide drains.

The other kind of slum upgradation involved moving people out to vacant lands where, under a World Bank scheme, developed sites—with water and electricity—were provided to them. Thereafter, they were left to build their own houses on these plots.

Even as different schemes were being devised and implemented, the 'cut-off' date for deciding which were 'recognized' slums and which were illegal changed every few years. It moved progressively from 1976, when the first census was done, to 1980, then 1985, and finally 1995 (at the time of writing).

Thus, when PMGP was launched, parts of Dharavi had already benefited partially from the slum improvement scheme and the slum upgradation scheme. But the benefits were limited to settlements on government or municipal land. The spatial layout of the settlements made the implementation of some of these schemes virtually impossible.

Gautam Chatterjee recalls, for instance, the difficulty of providing toilets to people living in parts of Dharavi. 'Because the slums in Dharavi are so dense, you are not in a position to give upgraded infrastructure. To give you an example, under the slum improvement programmes, we were supposed to provide one toilet for thirty-five heads. Under the slum upgradation programme, the norm was brought down to fifteen heads per toilet. But in actual practice, under the improvement programme, what we were able to achieve was one toilet for 100 heads. It was not possible to achieve the norm of thirty-five because of the density. You could not pull down existing residential structures in order to build toilets.'

Ironically, even today the only place to locate new toilets is in the middle of garbage dumps. Or if some open space is found to build a community toilet, the area around it inevitably becomes a garbage dump as there are precious few unencumbered areas.

One of the biggest problems slum-dwellers faced then, and still face, was accessing housing loans. Most people in slums live a precarious existence even if joint earnings of family members are enough to allow some to get consumer durables like television sets. A constant refrain of the uninformed middle classes is that if 'these' people can afford TVs—as is evident from the forest of antennae on the rooftops of most slum colonies—why can they not afford to live in 'proper' housing instead of squatting in this insanitary manner? They, of course, have no concept of the reality, that 'proper' housing was unavailable and unaffordable for the poor. Many slum-dwellers cannot find the money even to improve existing living structures. The state makes no provision for this.

Housing finance has been one of the endless problems that has haunted all housing schemes for the urban poor. Mainstream financial institutions are not equipped to deal with the kind of small loans at low interest rates that poor people require for their homes. Even if a group of them form a cooperative and apply for a loan from the existing housing finance institutions, the collateral requirements make such an application impossible to entertain. As a result, any improvement in their houses inevitably means taking loans from private loan sharks at usurious interest rates.

Thus, even if slum upgradation was lauded as a sensible scheme because it recognized the need of slum-dwellers to remain close to their place of work, it could not work as envisaged because the housing finance aspect of the scheme had not been worked out satisfactorily. The importance of this became even more acute in later schemes, such as slum redevelopment.

As a result, only slum households where one or more member had a secure job could muster up additional finances to improve their houses. Consequently, in the same slum, often in the same lane, you would find, side by side, improved structures and others that remained kaccha. In poorer areas, such self-generated improvements were clearly not possible.

Redeveloping slums

The PMGP was the first scheme that actually considered slum redevelopment, that is, planning for entirely new structures where slum-dwellers could live on the same site where they presently squatted. This was born out of a recognition that such reorganization was the only way to ensure real upgradation. Also, such redevelopment would free up land that could be used for other commercial purposes. The scheme also accepted the fact that people want to live where they can find work. Thus, the earlier concept of moving slum-dwellers to distant suburbs was acknowledged as being unworkable as people would merely abandon those dwellings and find their way back closer to work. Many previous slum improvement schemes had failed because the authorities had not understood the crucial link between work and a place to live, particularly in the absence of affordable public transport systems.

Chatterjee says he realized that the slum improvement or even slum upgradation programme would not give him enough schemes with which the Rs 37 crore allotted to Dharavi under PMGP could be spent. Of the total, Rs 17 crore was used for infrastructure, such as laying sewerage lines and widening roads. But given the density of the settlements, even the roads that were widened were those on the periphery of Dharavi. The exception was the 90 Feet Road, which runs through the middle of Dharavi and links the south to the north. Such a road already existed, but it had been so heavily encroached upon as to be unusable.

Under the PMGP, the encroachers were moved to a transit camp on one side of the road and the road was widened to something approximating 90 feet. Today, encroachers have once again reduced the width of the road to much less. But at least it is a usable road at most times of the year unlike Dharavi Main Road which remains narrow and highly congested.

Another Rs 2 crore of the PMGP was used to clean up the Mithi river which separates Dharavi from the northern suburbs of Mumbai. Since then, the river and the Mahim creek have become silted and increasingly polluted with unchecked dumping of construction debris. And the remaining Rs 18 crore was allocated for slum redevelopment.

Chatterjee realized that there was room for some innovation as existing approaches had proved inadequate in dealing with the problem. One idea that emerged was that of area development—to look at a cluster of settlements located in a particular part of Dharavi rather than individual settlements. An area adjacent to the newly widened 60 Feet Road, called Rajendra Prasad Nagar, was chosen. The majority of its residents had been relocated some decades earlier from Tardeo in central Mumbai.

Chatterjee decided to adopt a learning approach and began talking to the communities to find out what they really wanted. 'The people I spoke to argued that if dilapidated buildings could be repaired, why could there not be proper redevelopment of the slums. They wanted to get out of this so-called informal settlement syndrome and move to mainstream formal housing,' he says. 'This I thought was a brilliant idea because I would achieve my target of spending the money. The problem with upgradation was that with no space to construct toilets, you could not have spent the Rs 18 crore.' But this was easier said than done. For the government had still not accepted the concept of redevelopment—which means removing slums, temporarily, and rebuilding formal housing for them on the same plot. So far, the dominant approach towards slums was slum improvement and upgradation.

Fortunately for Chatterjee, he had the support of the then housing secretary, Dinesh K. Afzalpurkar (who coincidentally headed the committee which came up with the ambitious Slum Redevelopment Plan in 1995). Afzalpurkar issued a new government resolution which Chatterjee drafted. Under this, the beneficiaries would have to pay something towards their housing rather than getting it free as in the later scheme. The government recognized that the initial cost of redevelopment was outside the reach of poor people. 'So we developed a system by which we broke up these costs,' explains Chatterjee. The beneficiaries were expected to make a fixed initial contribution. A cross-subsidy was generated from commercial tenements which had to pay more. The difference between these two amounts was divided into monthly instalments which the beneficiaries were expected to pay over fifteen to twenty years.

Additionally, these monthly instalments would increase telescopically. In other words, families would begin by paying Rs 100 per month and then gradually, the monthly contributions would increase up to Rs 250. The normal size of an apartment for the Low Income Group (LIG) was 180 sq.ft of carpet area, costing about Rs 37,000. People were expected to pay two instalments of Rs 5,000 each, one as down payment and the other on completion. Around Rs 5,400 per tenement would be generated as cross-subsidy from commercial tenements on the ground floor. The remaining Rs 22,000 would be recovered from the people at 10 per cent rate of interest over a period of fifteen to twenty years.

On paper, the scheme sounded logical. In fact, it was not, for it created tremendous difficulties for the supposed beneficiaries primarily because the State did not take into account the investment that people had already made in their existing structures, often going into debt in the process. Instead, it wanted them to accept a further burden of debt for the new house.

Secondly, the scheme did not accommodate the additional servicing costs of living in these new apartment blocks. Even if the residents paid a 'rent' to the municipal corporation, if they lived on municipal land, or to the local dada, if it was private land, the amount was far lower than what they would be expected to pay in the new PMGP buildings. As a result, PMGP triggered off a panic sale of huts as people recovered the costs of improving their huts and moved into other slums.

Chatterjee grants that the difference between PMGP and previous government schemes was that it had built-in community consultation and participation. But the extent of such participation was limited to the community forming a society and appointing its own architect. 'Once that was done, the scheme was submitted to the PMGP. We would have to spend all the money and even the community's contribution would have to come to PMGP. We would then proceed, through the transparent bidding mechanism for contracts. The contractor's work would be supervised by the architect who would be accountable to the community. PMGP would also monitor the work and pay out the money. At the same time we had to spend money constructing transit camps.'

It is precisely this centralization of control with the PMGP that self-help groups found difficult to accept as it removed from their hands the control over the final construction of their buildings. Here Chatterjee differed with some of the community-based organizations already working in Dharavi. He admits that he had a different approach then. Since then, his views are more akin to those expressed by the non-governmental organizations in terms of what people want and need and how to ensure that their participation in slum redevelopment schemes is meaningful and sustainable.

People's way

In 1986, Chatterjee and his colleagues were working on a different set of premises than organizations like the National Slum Dwellers' Federation (NSDF) and Society for Promotion of Area Resource Centres (SPARC). NSDF/SPARC saw that the exercise to redevelop Dharavi was being done in the absence of a clear understanding of what Dharavi really is, or of what those who were expected to be a part of the scheme really wanted. To obtain more accurate information about the settlements that together made up Dharavi and to ascertain people's views on the redevelopment plan, NSDF/SPARC launched an enumeration exercise.

The Dharavi survey involved communities in different settlements in the process so that the information generated would be 'owned' by them and they could use it in their negotiations with the State in the future. Too often surveys of such areas are conducted without involving the people concerned. As a result, they have no idea why the information is being collected and to what use it will be put.

In the course of doing the enumeration, NSDF/ SPARC realized that although Dharavi was being looked upon as one slum even by the planners, the residents did not see themselves as part of one settlement. Instead, each settlement had a distinct identity. This was determined by the people who lived there—whether they had been relocated from another part of Mumbai, whether they were migrants from one part of India, or whether they were people involved in a common trade.

For the process of enumeration, people from each settlement were trained to gather the information. At the end of each day, the team of enumerators would collate the data and explain the process to the community so that the entire exercise was transparent and inclusive. The data was then cross-checked against the ration cards available at the local fair price shop and also the voters' list at the Election Commission's office, as well as the rent lists at the Collectorate. Regularized slum households with a photopass pay 'rent' regularly to the Collector. This is an important document to establish their identity and the length of time they have lived in a particular slum.

As a result of this exercise, people were able to develop their own map of Dharavi which marked out all the main landmarks. They also examined land records to determine the ownership of the land on which their settlements had been constructed. They found, for instance, that of the 175 hectares that made up Dharavi, 106 hectares belonged to the municipal corporation, private owners came next with 43 hectares and the rest was state or Central government land. It was in the course of the enumeration process that the Dharavi Vikas Samiti (Dharavi Development Committee) consisting of people interested in improving Dharavi, was established. It allied itself with the NSDF.

Even as the NSDF/SPARC team was involving communities in the enumeration and data collection process, the government decided to conduct its own survey for the PMGP scheme. Over 5,000 government representatives fanned out into the settlements to collect the information. In the end, there was a significant disparity between the numbers that the NSDF/SPARC survey produced and that of the government.

According to the government survey, there were 55,000 households in Dharavi in November 1987. The NSDF/SPARC survey counted 86,000 structures housing 1,06,000 families with an average of 6.2 individuals per house. In addition, they counted sixty-two Pongal houses.

If one accepted the NSDF/SPARC data, the

population of Dharavi would have been over six lakh in 1986. The PMGP was working on a figure of three lakh and the earlier Correa Committee had concluded that there were only 2.5 lakh people living in Dharavi.

Such a huge discrepancy in numbers underlines the inaccuracy of government-run surveys in areas like Dharavi, where people are not ready to tell you the full story unless they trust you. That is why the community-based approach to enumeration, so that the data would be in the hands of the community, made sense and was ultimately far more useful.

Unfortunately, the government continues to use its own inadequate and inaccurate data for all its plans without even looking at the reality. In Dharavi, you do not need to count each house to realize that the official numbers and the real numbers are vastly different.

Where they came from

One of the innovative aspects of the NSDF/SPARC survey was the 'historical trace'. They tried to locate the original residents of Dharavi and put together a picture of how it had grown and developed. This process revealed that many migrants had settled in Dharavi from the early 1930s, when this swampy stretch was at the edge of the city limits. In the 1950s, '60s and '70s, many pavement and slum-dwellers from the island city of Bombay were moved to Dharavi. The later migrants were those who came to join the existing trade activities in the settlements or to work in the city as the area was conveniently located between two major railway lines— Central and Western.

The survey also revealed the composition of Dharavi's

residents. The majority, 36.76 per cent, came from Tamil Nadu, closely followed by 33.36 per cent from Maharashtra. Other groups were from Uttar Pradesh, Karnataka, Andhra Pradesh, Gujarat, Kerala, Rajasthan and Bihar, in that order. Of the Tamilians, over half came from Tirunelvelli district; the other big chunk, more than a quarter, were from Salem. The rest of the Tamil population included people from South Arcot, North Arcot, Ramanathapuram, Kanyakumari, Madurai and Coimbatore districts.

Of the Maharashtrians, over 20 per cent were from Ratnagiri, closely followed by 19.24 per cent from Satara. There were also people from Sangli, Solapur, Kolhapur and Pune districts. The original inhabitants of Dharavi, the Kolis, were less than 6 per cent of the Marathi-speaking population.

Although people from Uttar Pradesh comprised only 10 per cent of the population, according to this survey, they are certainly as visible a presence in Dharavi as the Tamilians. Indeed, a casual observer might be led to believe that their numbers equal those of the Tamilians. However, this is not true. Their visibility has partly to do with the trades in which they are involved, like the leather business, and the fact that they live in large concentrations around Badi Masjid on Dharavi Main Road. One-third of the UP-wallahs come from Azamgarh district, another third from Basti and the rest from Gonda, Jaunpur, Faridabad, Lucknow, Allahabad and Pratapgarh.

The survey documented all the income-generating occupations in Dharavi and came up with an astoundingly varied list. This ranged from 5,000 units churning out leather finished goods to one of the largest plastic recycling industries in the country employing more than 5,000 people on daily wages. A thriving food industry produced everything—from idlis, to chiki, gulab jamuns, channa and papads—in the lanes and bylanes of Dharavi. And an estimated twenty-five bakeries sent out fresh pav, khari and butter to all parts of the city.

Also, according to the survey, while Dharavi had twenty-seven temples, six churches and eleven mosques, it had only 842 toilets and 162 taps for a population of six lakh. On completion of this exercise, and given the profile of Dharavi that emerged from it of a productive area where a large number of small industries thrived, NSDF argued that the PMGP should recognize that parts of Dharavi were industrial and should be granted that status instead of shifting out production units from the area.

The PMGP never got around to tackling the vast 13th Compound, the recycling centre of Dharavi, even though a fire in the area provided it with the ideal opportunity to start from scratch. At the same time, barring one instance where NSDF was central to the formation of a cooperative society, it failed to accept the concept of housing that accommodates petty trades which provide sustenance to the majority of people living in Dharavi.

PMGP concentrated instead on the periphery of Dharavi as these were the areas where the new sewer lines had been laid. As a result, it was feasible to build high-rises with toilets in the flats. Practically no work has been done since then to extend the sewer lines to the interior of Dharavi. High-rises have come up on all sides of Dharavi but the central part of the settlement remains dense, disorganized and unserviced.

Whatever its shortcoming, the PMGP scheme was a beginning. It marked the recognition of Dharavi as a potentially developable area. It also marked the start of an expansion phase in the city's development where an east-west axis was recognized as important. So far, most of the service sector had concentrated on the southern tip of the island city and the industry had been moved north under the development plan. Housing had increasingly grown in the northern suburbs with its proximity to employment. As a result, the transport services along this north-south axis were increasingly stretched and overused.

The idea of developing reclaimed land from the Mahim creek area just north of Dharavi began to take shape around the time the PMGP buildings were being constructed. Although several government buildings, including the Maharashtra Housing and Area Development Authority, had come up in the area, the idea got a fillip when the Diamond Bourse was proposed on land across the creek and the Bandra-Kurla complex of offices was planned. Suddenly, Dharavi's location became much more attractive.

Free houses

In 1996, Gautam Chatterjee found himself heading the Slum Redevelopment Authority (SRA) and was given the task of implementing a much more ambitious Slum Redevelopment Scheme (SRS) devised under the coalition government of the Shiv Sena and the Bharatiya Janata Party in 1995. In their election manifesto, these parties had promised free houses to 40 lakh slum households in Mumbai. It was argued that most slum-dwellers had already spent a substantial amount to develop the land on which they lived. Given the current value of that land, they ought to be given a free house in exchange for releasing some of the land for other uses.

The scheme, however, had to be fleshed out. The government set up a committee headed by Dinesh K. Afzalpurkar, who already had the experience of the PMGP, and invited private builders and some non-governmental organizations to join in.

The result was a scheme that, at least on paper, appeared workable. At the time the scheme was launched, land prices in Bombay had gone through the roof. The SRS expected that private builders would be interested in redeveloping slums if they could gain something out of it. Thus, the scheme permitted private builders to get the consent of 70 per cent of the residents of any slum, move them to temporary transit accommodation (which the government would build) and construct high-rise buildings on this land. These buildings would include those that accommodated the slum-dwellers, giving them a free flat each, and also buildings with bigger flats which could be sold on the open market, thereby allowing the builder to recover his costs and more.

Each slum household was promised a 225 sq.ft area free in these high-rises with a built-in toilet. However, the height of the room would be just 9 feet. As a result, those slum-dwellers who had already invested in a loft in their existing structures as part of the slum upgradation project did not find the scheme attractive. The scheme had a commercial component but only for recognized businesses. As most slum-dwellers conduct unrecognized business in their homes, they were not entitled to additional space where this could be done.

It was assumed that because the slum-dwellers were being offered a free house, they would jump at it. In fact, as the director of SPARC, Sheela Patel, argues, over a lifetime most slum-dwellers would have spent up to Rs 2 lakh to upgrade their existing dwellings. So the replacement is technically not free. Furthermore, the monthly outgoings for maintenance are often higher than what they pay presently by way of 'rent'.

The SRS failed to take off not just because of a lack of enthusiasm amongst some slum communities but also because of the fall in land prices within a year of the scheme being launched. When the plan was finalized in 1995, land prices in Mumbai were high. Dharavi's current location made it an especially attractive place for implementing the scheme. It is sandwiched conveniently between Western and Central Railway. And just across the Mahim creek, which cannot be reclaimed because it has been declared an ecologically important area, is the new Diamond Bourse which is being developed. A little further is the Mangaldas Goculdas Market that is eventually tipped to replace the centuries old Crawford Market in south Mumbai.

It was assumed that once these two schemes took off, many a merchant would want living/office space much closer to these locations. Dharavi would be ideal, specially the areas running alongside the main Mahim-Sion link road. Dreaming of making a killing, builders moved into Dharavi as soon as the SRS was announced, quickly rounded up slum-dwellers, and got them to agree to form societies. Scores of redevelopment schemes were rapidly formulated and cleared by the authority. Money passed hands, societies were registered, commencement certificates were issued, some of the old houses were demolished and the residents sent off to transit camps. And then nothing happened.

By the time all this had been done, the market had crashed. The development of the Bandra-Kurla complex also slowed down. Suddenly, redeveloping Dharavi was not such a lucrative proposition for private builders. The profit margin was nowhere near the earlier calculations. Right across Dharavi you find evidence of the greed of private builders and the disappointment of the area's residents.

As a result, even genuine schemes were looked upon sceptically. According to Jockin, who has fought for years for the housing rights of the urban poor, 30 to 35 per cent of all societies formed on paper in Dharavi are dysfunctional.

One group broke through this scepticism and that was the Dharavi Vikas Samiti (DVS) which is a part of NSDF. The federation's approach to the SRS is entirely pragmatic. They view it as an opportunity for communities to fight for the kind of housing they feel they need and, at the same time, take the entitlement that the State is giving them. Rather than either spurning the scheme because of the many problem areas in it, or handing over their future housing to a private builder, members of DVS, with the help of NSDF, decided to negotiate with the government for some critical changes in the scheme.

An earlier attempt to do this had failed. DVS had tried, when buildings were being constructed under the PMGP, to design and redevelop one area where their members lived. They designed a building which accommodated the needs of families for a loft by getting the government to agree that the rooms would have a height of 14 feet even though the regulation height is only 10 feet. Consultations with members of the community revealed that the majority were happy to have a community toilet as they did not want to waste precious space in their rooms. Under the PMGP schemes, the houses were only 180 sq.ft for the low-income groups. And most people did not want a building of more than ground plus one as they were concerned about how far they would need to walk in the eventuality, or inevitability, of water shortage. These were practical points that had emerged from detailed consultations with the community.

Unfortunately, in the 1980s, when DVS and NSDF attempted this intervention, they had not mastered the system of housing finance. As a result, a scheme that was billed to take no more than two years, dragged on for ten, adding to costs and the frustration of members of the society. The building was finally completed, but it did not resemble its original plan because the society had to make changes to accommodate many more households to recover the costs.

The experience of what is called Markandaya Society under PMGP, had prepared the Dharavi Vikas Samiti to deal with the Slum Redevelopment Scheme. P.S. Shanmuganand, originally from Tirunelvelli district, is the chief developer of the Rajiv Indira Cooperative Housing Society. Located off the main Mahim-Sion link road in Kalyanwadi, this building has become the cynosure of all eyes in Dharavi.

The reasons are simple. DVS first got all the fifty-four residents of the plot to agree to form a society which they themselves would manage. Then they found a contractor who would do the work. They were lucky.

They found four brothers, who own and run Falak Construction Pvt. Ltd., who readily agreed to take on the task.

DVS negotiated with the Slum Redevelopment Authority, under which all the schemes are managed, for a special dispensation; they wanted to construct flats of 225 sq.ft, as required under the scheme, but with a height of 14 feet which would permit a half-loft. They argued that this would ensure that all those with workshops in their homes could continue their work and even those who did not do so at present, would find a source of additional income.

The permission was granted and today, Markandaya Society in the south of Dharavi, on 60 Feet Road, and Rajiv Indira Cooperative Housing Society on the highway, have this arrangement. A three-plus-ground building will accommodate the fifty-four families. In the additional area, freed by removing their huts, another building will be constructed of seven floors with the regular 9 feet high, 225 sq.ft flats. This will accommodate another forty-two families from an adjoining slum. This scheme, in turn, will free up space near the road, give Rajiv Indira Housing Society better access to the main road, and allow them to develop the roadside property as commercial premises which can be sold at good prices.

The scheme is innovative because it accommodates people's needs and also recognizes the commercial possibilities that this location can yield. The Rajiv Indira Housing Society example has now been accepted as a feasible plan that any group of slum-dwellers can adopt as part of the redevelopment scheme.

Lessons for the future

There are several lessons from the Rajiv Indira Cooperative Society experience that are relevant for future slum redevelopment schemes in Mumbai or elsewhere. First, if a community is consulted, and assured that its views will be taken seriously, there is the possibility of coming up with housing solutions that people want and will maintain. In the past, government-designed and funded housing schemes for the urban poor have been deemed failures because the 'beneficiaries' have sold their allotted flats and moved back into slums.

The assumption from this was that such people prefer to live in illegal, informal housing rather than in formal housing. It has never been considered that the kind of structures the government has built for the poor are inappropriate. Most of these buildings are not just badly designed but are also poorly constructed. If you have four-storey-high buildings without an adequate water supply and built-in toilets, how are people supposed to survive? Without water, flushes do not work. And no one, not even a poor person, will voluntarily want to carry water up four floors just for the joy of living in a pucca building which looks as if it is about to collapse. Furthermore, as it is mostly women who have to bear the burden of collecting water, they are hardly going to be enthusiastic about such structures. They would much prefer living in their incrementally improved ground-level slum structures.

Dharavi today has several buildings which are either unfinished or which have been caught up in disputes, lying empty and unused, while their neighbourhoods are teeming with people waiting for a pucca house. These are the buildings constructed under various schemes including the PMGP. They were supposed to be 'sold' to raise additional finance for low-cost housing. But neither did buyers rush to purchase flats which were so poorly constructed, nor were they allocated to people in Dharavi looking for a place to live.

This is a pity, as unlike many other areas, people living in Dharavi wish to continue living there. This is evident from the composition of people living in the high-rises built on private lands like the Nagri and Diamond Apartments as well as Vaibhav. Most of the residents of these buildings are people who had always lived in Dharavi. This shows a certain level of identification with the area which you do not necessarily find in other slums. It also suggests that if buildings meet the needs of the people who plan to live in them, irrespective of whether they are poor or rich, they are likely to remain occupied, and will even be maintained, than unimaginative concrete blocks constructed in haste to solve a 'problem'.

The Dharavi experience also shows the limitations of seeing areas as 'slums' without recognizing the variegated nature of land use and structures. People live in Dharavi, but they also work there. In the absence of separate areas for production units, the two are merged. While this might not matter much for home-based industries, it is a real health hazard in the case of other units. There are units, for instance, that have furnaces built into the rooms. Men work and breathe vast quantities of carbon monoxide day and night. In other parts, bakeries light their wood-fired ovens in the early hours of the morning and the entire area is enveloped in choking smoke. And the filthy work of treating leather hides, which includes washing off the blood and flesh and later removing the hair, is conducted in open spaces in close proximity to where people live. All this muck flows down open drains, past people's homes.

Under the present scheme, the high-rises will provide places for people to live and there will be some commercial spaces, mainly for shops. But there is no plan for the small-scale industries that are such an integral part of a place like Dharavi.

There are two strategies that can be adopted. One is to close down all hazardous units, regardless of where they are located, and move them out of Dharavi. In the past, such a strategy did not work in the oldest industry of Dharavi, leather processing. It will be even more difficult in the case of small production units which are hidden deep inside the dense settlements. But a systematic effort could be made. The new location need not be in a distant suburb. There are several plots of land alongside the Mahim-Sion link road which could be developed into mini-industrial areas. In fact, 13th Compound, which is a vast recycling area, is ideally located for such a purpose.

For the non-polluting units, a separate strategy needs to be devised. These businesses run on very low margins. Often all the members of a household are employed in the work. Such businesses could not survive if people are required to pay additional costs for a place where the work is done. A more pragmatic approach is to accept the argument put forward by the Rajiv Indira

Cooperative Society, that is, to permit a loft to be constructed as part of the 225 sq.ft room in some buildings. People have expressed their willingness to pay for this additional space. In the long run, a genuine and sustainable redevelopment of a place like Dharavi is only possible if the working needs of the people are fully accommodated.

And, finally, what Dharavi shows is that the needs of settlements vary greatly. Therefore, a uniform approach to redevelopment is not feasible. The potters of Kumbharwada, for instance, will not be satisfied with a high-rise building, even if their rooms have a half-loft because their trade requires space at ground level for their potters' wheels and their kilns.

Therefore, instead of treating all of Dharavi like one slum and imposing a uniform policy, flexibility and real community consultation needs to be built into the policy. This will ensure that people will take some initiative in solving their housing problem instead of sitting back and waiting for the government to deliver.

Dharavi is already greatly transformed from the days when people spoke of it as a *khadi* (swamp). 'Now it is *sona*,' says Khatija remembering her early days in Dharavi. 'Then there was no electricity. We used to live on that *khadi* and there, day and night, the *daru ka bhatti* would be burning. When I first saw it, I thought the entire hill was on fire!'

At the end of 1999, Dharavi had moved a long distance from the days of burning hills and swamps. But Khatija continues to live in Dargah Chawl, Social Nagar, albeit in a greatly improved structure. She still dreams of a pucca house.

6

Many More Dharavis

Ayesha Taleyarkhan

On one of my visits to Dharavi while researching this book, I had an encounter that has stayed with me. I had parked my car on a dirt patch on 90 Feet Road opposite the police station. When I came back, after meeting a group of Dalits from Karnataka and Andhra Pradesh, I found that one of the tyres was flat. I looked around for some help and, as if out of nowhere, two little boys were at my elbow. They looked no older than eight. Their names were Raju and Abbas.

I asked them where they came from. Dharavi, said one. Chembur, said the other. On further inquiry, it transpired that Raju was a 'Madrasi' and Abbas' family was originally from Azamgarh. But neither 'Madras' nor Azamgarh had any meaning for these 'Bombay boys' as they expertly changed the tyre and went off beaming with my tip in their hands. They were singing a popular Hindi film song as they walked towards the garage where they worked.

I often think of Raju and Abbas and wonder what will happen to the thousands like them who always toil and sometimes flourish amidst the dirt and the chaos of Dharavi's lanes. A generation has grown up in places like Dharavi who know no other home except Mumbai. Their role models in these informal settlements are often their own 'bosses', who began like them and are now owners. This book contains only a handful of Dharavi's many success stories which inspire successive generations.

What will Dharavi be like by the time Raju and Abbas become maliks? It is entirely possible that by the year 2010, Dharavi as we know it today will be just a memory. Instead of the current medley of disorganized low-rise high density huts and a few scattered high-rises, the entire area could become another typical concrete conclave of high-rises. Given the rate of change in many parts of Mumbai, such a transformation should not take anyone by surprise.

One only has to drive through the old textile mill district of the city—which until the beginning of the 1980s was a bustling industrial area—to see how cities change. Today, the majority of the textile mills—once the pride of Mumbai—are ghost-like, neglected, skeletal structures. Some mills have constructed high-rise residential buildings on their land. Apartments in these buildings are out of reach for the textile workers who continue to live in dilapidated chawls elsewhere. Office buildings have also sprung up in the compounds of former textile mills. Only multinationals and leading advertising agencies can afford these office spaces. And upmarket restaurants, discotheques, art galleries and amusement arcades for the rich have proliferated.

If some of the profits from these new developments had been invested in providing alternative employment, better housing and facilities for the thousands of unemployed textile workers in Mumbai, perhaps the dissonance would not have been so great. But the style of redevelopment that Mumbai's mill lands have seen attempts to erase the past, to wipe away history, and to reduce it to symbols by maintaining the old facade of buildings to hide the disjunction with the new reality inside them.

Dharavi, in particular, faces similar pressures as do the mill lands because of its important location. Land in no other 'slum' in Mumbai is quite as coveted as is this former swamp. Dharavi's central location makes it ideal for the kind of gentrification the mill area of Mumbai has seen. Even as I write this last chapter, there is news of more developments in the Bandra-Kurla area, across the creek from Dharavi. The latest is a mega entertainment centre which will have eight cinema theatres and as many upmarket restaurants. All these developments make Dharavi even more attractive as a location for residential and office buildings.

The question that will determine whether the Dharavi of the future will have any relation to the Dharavi of the past and the present depends on several important factors. The most crucial is how the government chooses to deal with the enterprises—legal and illegal—that flourish in Dharavi.

One option is to close them down, regardless of size or mode of production. If such a decision is actually implemented—so far decisions to move out polluting industries have only been imposed half-heartedly—Dharavi's essential profile will change from commercial/industrial to only residential. This will inevitably lead to a change in the population profile. For if the policy to stop any kind of industrial production, small or large, is actually implemented, the people who will be affected will not only be the owners of these enterprises but also the people who work in them. The owners will have the money to be able to continue to live in Dharavi even if their production unit is moved elsewhere. Indeed, many of those who have done well for themselves in Dharavi have continued to live there in privately-constructed high-rises.

The people who will suffer most from this decision are the workers in these enterprises. Thousands of workers in Dharavi, in the garment and leather industry and in the food industry, live and work in the same place. It is these people, who actually do not 'own' anything in Dharavi, who will be displaced once the informal industries are moved out. They will have no choice but to move where these enterprises shift.

Another alternative, which had been suggested earlier by the NSDF and the Dharavi Vikas Samiti, is to develop a part of Dharavi as a non-polluting production centre. This will allow at least some of the small businesses, such as garments, or leather finished goods, or even some food production units, to continue in Dharavi. Also, as several communities have demanded, if the new buildings are allowed rooms which can accommodate a half-loft, a number of the home-based businesses will survive.

On the other hand, if Dharavi is converted into a purely residential area, many of its existing residents will be tempted to sell out and move elsewhere as they have no other capital but their photopass. Inevitably, people will sell their huts, or their apartments in the new buildings and look for cheaper accommodation further away from the city centre. Thus, the story of the past, of constant movement from developed to undeveloped areas, will continue.

Such future developments would not be dissimilar to what is already happening in the mill areas of Mumbai. Here too, old houses and chawls are gradually giving way to new buildings where the middle classes are moving in. Tenants of these chawls, many of them unemployed textile workers, are using this as an opportunity to build up some capital as they have nothing else which they can capitalize on.

As the population profile of these areas changes, so will the quality of services. Gentrification will inevitably mean pressure to improve infrastructure, such as water supply, sewerage and garbage clearance. Already, upmarket restaurants are positioning themselves closer to these new developments. The inequalities of the past will replay themselves; as areas get peopled with those with resources, the authorities respond. As long as the population is poor, the areas remain neglected.

One could argue that such change is inevitable in cities. It would be acceptable if it did not increase hardships for those who have actually developed the areas and made them what they are today.

'Pull Down' syndrome

One often hears middle-class people say that the government should 'pull down' Dharavi and then redevelop it. The thinking behind such statements is frightening because it treats a place like Dharavi as if it were a structure, a few buildings, and not people with lives and aspirations like anyone else. It is suggestive of the blindness that even the thought of a slum seems to induce in the middle class. The ugliness of the structures is all that people see, not the vitality of those who live in these tenements. As a result, people glibly talk about slum removal and city beautification without a thought to the dislocation and anguish that this causes to thousands of families.

It is true that in some instances, given the spatial layout of slums, there is no option but to pull down existing structures and start afresh. Many slum-dwellers want this. But as long as the redevelopment accommodates the original occupants of the land on which the new structures are being constructed, there is no problem. The tragedy is that most often redevelopment results in forcing out the people for whom it is intended, either because the design of the new buildings is not suited to the needs of the poor, or because the outgoings are too steep for people with minimum surplus funds.

This book describes the gradual change in attitude towards slums as reflected in the government's policy. This has moved from slum removal, to slum improvement, upgradation and, finally, redevelopment. Yet, despite the introduction of programmes that acknowledge the rights of people living in slums, some things have not changed. Governments still do not acknowledge that poor people have a fundamental right to decent housing and that it is the responsibility of the State to enable them to get it. This can be the only explanation for the ease with which the government regresses into a policy of demolitions and slum removal, something that on paper had been discarded in the 1970s.

Mumbai had not seen large-scale demolitions of slums in many decades. But the first few months of the year 2000 will be remembered for the renewed rash of demolitions that pushed out thousands of families from homes in which they had lived for decades.

On 28 February 2000, hundreds of houses that had stood within a few feet of the rail tracks for over two decades were razed to the ground. Overnight, 2,360 families were rendered homeless. The demolition drive by the railways was in response to a public interest litigation (PIL) filed in the Bombay High Court by a group of middle-class citizens. They were moved to act when commuters travelling on the city's impossibly packed suburban rail network were injured by stones thrown at them as the trains passed these slums.

There was no clear proof that the people throwing the stones were those who lived in these slums. No one could explain why people, who live just three feet away from the tracks and daily risk life and limb, would want to continue to stay there or why they should hurl stones all of a sudden at trains which pass their houses every few minutes throughout the day. But the issue became a highly emotive one as newspapers carried photographs of innocent travellers who had been grievously injured by these stones. People also read stories of how the railways were hamstrung to improve the services because they could not afford to run the trains fast along tracks where people lived on either side, sometimes within touching distance. Something clearly had to be done.

The irony of this particular situation is that something was being done. Railway slum-dwellers had formed societies and savings groups to put aside money for housing and had been negotiating with the railways and the government for alternative land. The Harbour Line had been extended to Navi Mumbai without a struggle because the slum-dwellers who came in the way of the expansion had peacefully, and happily, shifted to a plot of land on the other side of the highway made available for them. They had designed their own housing, and paid for a part of it.

Yet, sadly, despite proof that people wanted to help themselves and that the process could be achieved without violence or resistance, the anxiety to show instant results led to these demolitions. The irony was greater still as the people living along railway tracks, and pavement dwellers, had finally succeeded in getting themselves 'recognized' by the government. As a result, under the Maharashtra government's Slum Redevelopment Scheme (SRS), if they could prove their stay in the same plot before 1 January 1995, they were entitled to alternative accommodation. All these formulations fell by the wayside as the bulldozers, under media glare, razed dwellings on either side of the tracks.

Unlike the protests in 1981, when the shelters of pavement dwellers had been bulldozed at the height of the monsoon, no human rights group intervened this time. The demolitions stopped only after the NSDF and senior bureaucrats who had supported the process of resettlement that was under way called a halt. But the demolitions were an ugly reminder of the fragility of the slum-dwellers' existence.

Fortunately, some good did come out of this tragedy. Several hundred of the displaced, who could prove that they had lived on the same plot before 1 January 1995 and were thus entitled to free alternative accommodation in the event of a demolition, were given keys to flats that had already been constructed by government agencies as public housing. These buildings had been built to resettle slum-dwellers but had not been allocated to any group in particular.

If the government had not decided to move the railway slum-dwellers to these buildings, it is possible that they would have remained unoccupied for several months, perhaps even years. Many buildings remain empty because the government cannot decide whether they should be used for rehousing slum-dwellers or whether the government should try and recover its investment by selling the tenements in the open market. The latter strategy is rarely successful as most of these buildings are too shabby for the market and too expensive for the poor.

In the case of the resettled railway slum-dwellers, the railways and the state government arrived at an agreed formula to pay for the tenements. This formula has now been used to voluntarily resettle people living on land belonging to the Indian Navy and the Airports Authority of India. The latter effort has freed an important runway at Mumbai's airport which could not be used because of its proximity to the slum.

Environment vs. slums

Another arena for bulldozer action did not see such a happy ending. This was on the question of the future of some 33,000 slum households (the unofficial figure is 55,000 households—an estimated 3 lakh people) who had encroached on land that was part of the Sanjay Gandhi National Park in Borivili, a Mumbai suburb. This is an important nature reserve for Mumbai as two of the lakes that provide water to the city are located within it. But these lakes are a long way from the outer edges of the park where the encroachments have taken place.

The forest department claims it was helpless to deal with the encroachments in the past because slum-dwellers always managed to get a stay order through the courts or got the government or a politician to intervene on their behalf. Slum-dwellers claim that the forest department constantly harassed them but did nothing about other illegalities that were taking place in the park.

In the middle of this stand-off, an environmental group filed a writ in the high court asking that the laws relating to national parks be implemented and the court accepted their argument. As a result, thousands of families faced demolition squads. The court had given people time to put a down payment and move to a location that was quite a distance away. When the extended deadline ran out, the court refused to halt the demolitions.

The battle was a classic one between those who feel strongly that guarding the environment safeguards everyone's interests, and those who feel that the interests of the poor ought to be primary. A middle way could have been attempted whereby some redevelopment could have been done *in situ*. Some people could have been relocated but not so far that they would be displaced from their employment. Unfortunately, with polarized positions on both sides, such a halfway compromise was not possible.

Also joining battle against these slum-dwellers were

a group of middle-class citizens who wanted to clean up their neighbourhood. There is practically no neighbourhood in Mumbai, barring very few, where a slum does not exist somewhere close by. People living in these slums work as domestics and drivers in middle-class homes and in upmarket buildings. Yet those who employ them do not feel any sense of responsibility for their living conditions or their future.

These citizens' groups have now been demanding that the slums in their neighbourhoods be removed, holding them responsible for the dirt and the crime. The courts have responded, once again, to these demands and the demolition squads have moved in. While an active citizenry will aid a city in many ways, people who refuse to acknowledge the reality of poverty in a rich city like Mumbai are planting the seeds of social unrest that will inevitably affect everyone.

These incidents, which have pitted environmentalists and middle-class citizens' groups against poor people in Mumbai, underline the urgent need to arrive at some kind of workable formula to deal with the housing needs of poor people. For apart from dealing with the slums that already exist, there are new ones coming up all the time. What do you do about this? Some people suggest that the police and the municipality should maintain a constant vigil and ruthlessly destroy all such new slums. But is this an answer? People will just move somewhere else as they have done in the past. Dharavi's story illustrates only too well how it grew because people were pushed out of other parts of the city.

The influx of poor people into a city like Mumbai cannot be checked unless larger issues of development are addressed. India's current development course is forcing people in rural areas off agricultural land and into urban areas because small landholdings are unviable, or because of forced displacement through large projects such as dams or other infrastructure projects. Resettlement and rehabilitation plans in such instances have rarely been adequate. As a result, the displaced inevitably make their way to cities and join the burgeoning ranks of people in the informal sector of the urban economy.

Lessons from Dharavi

Given this reality, there is no getting away from the need to urgently, and realistically, address the housing needs of the urban poor. Here the story of a place like Dharavi should prove instructive for a number of reasons.

One, it illustrates how the most important issue is security of tenure. If poor people have that, they will generate the funds and find ways to improve their own structures. Once the government launched programmes that guaranteed people security, they were willing to redevelop their areas, or upgrade their dwellings. Even without any aid from the government, one can see how people have successfully replaced thatch and bamboo with brick and mortar. However, they cannot do anything about infrastructure. This has to be provided by the State.

Second, the process and manner in which slums are reorganized or redeveloped have to be done in consultation with the people involved. The stories from Dharavi show us that poor people are survival artists.

They are remarkable architects because within their restricted spaces, they have designed the use of space in ways that few trained architects could.

Non-governmental organizations working with the urban poor have long urged that women in particular must be involved in the planning and design of redeveloped slum settlements. People know what they need and they will be able to design something that is functional and can be maintained. There is enough evidence of dysfunctional 'people's housing' to suggest that a more open and consultative process is needed. In Dharavi, there are already a few examples, like the Rajiv Indira Cooperative in Kalyanwadi, which show what is possible when a community is consulted on all aspects of slum redevelopment.

Three, mainstream institutions of finance have rarely considered the needs of the poor. While the Maharashtra government's plan to provide free housing to slum-dwellers is commendable because it recognizes the investment that most of them have already made in their housing, it need not be the course for the future. If financial institutions can aid the poor in their housing needs, many slum-dwellers would be prepared to go part of the way in financing their housing. This is particularly true of a growing segment of slum-dwellers in Mumbai who are making small regular savings. There are literally hundreds of savings groups in the city that have been putting aside small amounts each month for their future housing needs. Such a savings movement can be upscaled if it is matched by the availability of formal housing finance.

Finally, places like Dharavi flourish because people

find work. They attract people because they embody the spirit of enterprise and survival in the face of tremendous obstacles. Architects, engineers and urban planners think of structures, but do not address the lives of people. As a result dream townships are planned which do not fulfil anyone's dreams. Livelihood and shelter have to be seen as one rather than separate entities.

Boys like Raju and Abbas have not come from anywhere, they are not going anywhere else. Mumbai is where they are from, Mumbai is where they will stay. Can a city survive if it ignores the needs of these boys, who represent more than half its citizens? The first step in our effort to find a solution to what seems a complex issue must necessarily be to stop, look, and listen.

References

Most of the material in this book is based on interviews the writer conducted with people in Dharavi and with officials who were involved at some stage in Dharavi's development. It also quotes from unpublished surveys by the National Slum Dwellers' Federation. Given below are other references, some of which have been quoted in the book.

Chaplin, Susan E., 'Cities, Sewers and Poverty: India's Politics of Sanitation', in *Environment and Urbanization*, Vol. II Number 1, April 1999.

Chodankar, Smita Raghunath, *Dharavi: From Shelter to Home*, Society for Human and Environmental Development (SHED), 1994.

Dossal, Mariam, 'Signatures in Space: Land Use In Colonial Bombay', in *Bombay: Metaphor For Modern India*, eds. Sujata Patel and Alice Thorner, Oxford University Press, 1995.

Jacobs, Jane, *The Death and Life of Great American Cities*, Vintage, 1961.

Panwalkar, Pratima, 'Upgradation of Slums: A World Bank Programme', in *Bombay: Metaphor for Modern India*, op. cit.

Pendse, Sandeep, 'Toil, Sweat and the City', op. cit.

Ribeiro, Julio, *Bullet for Bullet: My Life As a Police Officer*, Penguin Books India, 1998.

Seabrook, Jeremy, *Life and Labour in a Bombay Slum*, Quartet Books, 1987.

Srikrishna, Justice B.N., Report of the Srikrishna Commission, appointed for inquiry into the riots at Mumbai during December 1992-January 1993 and the 12 March 1993 bomb blasts.

Swaminathan, Madhura, 'Aspects of Urban Poverty in Bombay', in *Environment and Urbanization*, Vol. 7 Number 1, April 1995.

Tindall, Gillian, *City of Gold, The Biography of Bombay*, Penguin Books India, 1992.

Index